The Pocket

DEER
HUNTING
GUIDE

Successful Hunting with a Rife or Shotgun

by Stephen D. Carpenteri

Stoeger Publishing
Great Outdoor Books Since 1924

STOEGER PUBLISHING COMPANY
is a division of Benelli U.S.A.

Benelli U.S.A.
Vice President and General Manager:
 Stephen Otway
Vice President of Marketing and Communications:
 Stephen McKelvain

Stoeger Publishing Company
President: Jeffrey Reh
Publisher: Jennifer Thomas
Managing Editor: Harris J. Andrews
Creative Director: Cynthia T. Richardson
Graphic Designer: William Graves
Special Accounts Manager: Julie Brownlee
Publishing Assistant: Stacy Logue

Illustration: William Graves
Proofreader: Amy Jones

Published 2007 by:
Stoeger Publishing Company
17603 Indian Head Highway, Suite 200
Accokeek, Maryland 20607

BK0611
ISBN-13: 978-0-88317-331-2
ISBN-10: 0-88317-331-X
Library of Congress Control Number:
 2006925254

Manufactured in the United States of America.

*Distributed to the book trade and
to the sporting goods trade by:*
Stoeger Industries
17603 Indian Head Highway, Suite 200
Accokeek, Maryland 20607
301 283-6300   Fax: 301 283-6986
www.stoegerpublishing.com

OTHER PUBLICATIONS:

Shooter's Bible
 The World's Standard
 Firearms Reference Book

Gun Trader's Guide
 Complete Fully Illustrated
 Guide to Modern Firearms
 with Current Market Values

Hunting & Shooting:
The Bowhunter's Guide
Elk Hunter's Bible
High Performance Muzzleloading
 Big Game Rifles
High Power Rifle Accuracy:
 Before You Shoot
Hunt Club Management Guide
The Hunter's Journal
Hunting Tough Bucks
Hunting Whitetails East & West
Hunting the Whitetail Rut
Modern Shotgunning
Shotgunning for Deer
Taxidermy Guide
Trailing the Hunter's Moon
Whitetail Strategies

Firearms:
Antique Guns:
 A Collector's Guide
Beretta Pistols:
 the Ultimate Guide
Firearms Disassembly
 with Exploded Views
Guns & Ammo:
 The Shooter's Guide to
 Classic Firearms
Gunsmithing Made Easy
How to Buy & Sell Used Guns
Model 1911: Automatic Pistol
Modern Beretta Firearms

Reloading:
The Handloader's Manual of
 Cartridge Conversions 3rd Ed.

Fishing:
Big Bass Zone
Catfishing: Beyond the Basics
The Crappie Book
Fishing Made Easy
Fishing Online:
 1,000 Best Web Sites
Flyfishing for Trout A-Z
Out There Fishing
Practical Bowfishing
Walleye Pro's Notebook

Cooking Game:
The Complete Book of
 Dutch Oven Cooking
Dress 'Em Out
Wild About Freshwater Fish
Wild About Game Birds
Wild About Seafood
Wild About Venison
Wild About Waterfowl
World's Best Catfish Cookbook

Nature:
U.S. Guide to Venomous
 Snakes and Their Mimics

Pocket Guides:
The Pocket
 Disaster Survival Guide
The Pocket
 First-Aid Field Guide
The Pocket
 Fishing Basics Guide
The Pocket
 Outdoor Survival Guide

Fiction:
The Hunt
Wounded Moon

Nonfiction:
Escape In Iraq:
 The Thomas Hamill Story

*Dedicated to the unsung majority of deer hunters
who find their own spots, do their own scouting,
hunt on their own time, judge their own trophies
and eat the game they shoot.
Bravo!*

CONTENTS

Over the last 45 years I have visited countless tagging stations, meat packers and neighborhood deer processors as part of my job as an outdoor writer, and the one constant that stands out is that most of the deer being shot by hunters are does, yearlings, spike bucks or relatively small branch-antlered bucks. To me, these are all beautiful deer; excellent trophies with a great story behind them, and each one will provide many delicious meals for months to come. Hunters of all ages around the country see these deer, decide they are just what they are looking for and pull the trigger with great satisfaction. These hunters have their own measure of what constitutes a "trophy" deer, and for most of them it's the buck or doe they bring home at the end of the hunt.

I have also visited countless hunting camps from Maine to Florida, Maryland to Washington. The one constant is that every hunter in the house is happy to fill his tag, not necessarily with the new state-record buck or a world-class trophy, just a good, representative deer. For these hearty souls, it's not about proving their manhood or one-upping the guy in the next bunk, it's about being out there, enjoying the great outdoors, and coming home with enough stories and meat to last till next season. It's for these hunters that this book is written.

I killed my first deer, a small crotch-horn buck, using a Mossberg Model 395K bolt-action shotgun with buckshot and slugs — the deer was only three steps away at high noon! It was October 1963, and

I was strolling lazily down a Maine logging road with my shotgun over my shoulder, a can of Pepsi in my hand, ambling along on my way to meet up with Dad, who had walked on up the road ahead of me in search of tracks, rubs and other signs. I amused myself by listening to the incessant chatter of red squirrels and the occasional flush of a grouse which, in those days, seemed to be everywhere.

Suddenly I heard a shot, far up on the ridge to the west. I thought nothing of it. I heard another shot, closer this time, and thought nothing of it. I heard branches crackling and leaves crunching, and thought nothing of it. When a buck suddenly appeared before me, 10 yards away, ready to bound across the road, I finally thought something of it! I put my soda can down in the road, unslung my shotgun, aimed and — I'd forgotten to flip off the safety! I brought the gun down again, pushed the safety to "fire," aimed again, pulled the trigger and hit the buck square in the throat with a load of 00 buckshot. He went down like a sack of grain, kicking and thrashing.

I remembered Dad's advice: "If he keeps kicking, keep shooting!" I bolted in another load of buckshot, took careful aim ... and missed! I bolted in a third shell, a slug this time, took careful aim behind the deer's ear ... and just like that I had my first whitetail. Not a trophy? I beg to differ!

Looking back, I had done everything wrong a hunter could do under the circumstances, yet for some reason things worked out. I was king of deer camp that night. My first buck was gutted and hung in the big maple outside our cabin door by nightfall thanks to the assistance of some seasoned hunters from the camp below us (the ones who had missed the buck  on his fateful way into my lap). There was fried liver and onions for dinner and reminiscing about everyone's great hunting exploits for dessert. I could not have been happier and the events of that day have brought me back to the woods every fall since then. The sole purpose of this book is to put you in that picture this season, too!

If you're planning on going deer hunting this year, please don't do what I did! The odds of seeing a buck at noon on a warm day while walking idly down the road with your gun over your shoulder drinking soda are slim. There are better, more predicable ways to fill your tag. Stranger things certainly happen every year, but you can't trust every buck to blind luck!

Follow the simple suggestions in this book and you will increase your odds for success. No one can guarantee you a deer every year (whitetails are the toughest of all big game to fool on a regular basis), but our goal is to help you eliminate the common mistakes that keep those big, white tails waving goodbye each season!

THE PSYCHOLOGY OF DEER HUNTING

There are two major reasons why deer hunting success rates continue to hover around the 10% mark. You would think that with all of the incredible improvements in clothing, guns, scopes, ammunition, knowledge of deer habits — not to mention the increase in deer population — that it would be a cinch to go out, find and kill a deer. Amazingly enough, the opposite is true. I am editor of four popular outdoor magazines and the number of "my first deer" photos sent in by hunters in their 30s, 40s and older are astounding to me. They have hunted for years, they have the best of guns and gear, but somehow it took them half a lifetime or more to tag their first whitetail.

Get Out There!

I believe I know why, and the basic reasons are ridiculously simple: They don't go hunting often enough, and they miss what they shoot at!

I have hunted deer East and West, North and South with hunters of all ages and experience, and it doesn't matter if the hunt is taking place on the family farm or in the wild mountains of Montana, there is always someone in camp who won't get out of bed in the morning. The excuses are legion: "I'm tired," "I stayed up too late last night," "I drank too much," "I don't feel good," "It's raining," the list goes on.

I have left many a hunter, young and old, back in camp when I went out the door alone in the pre-dawn, but I thoroughly enjoyed their company hours later when, after their nap, they were called on to help me drag my trophy out of the woods.

Half the battle in deer hunting is going! Yes, it will be cold, wet, windy, hot, humid, dark, rainy, snowy — after all, it's deer season. Forget the excuses! Push yourself out of bed every day and spend every available hour in the woods. You won't see deer every minute of every day, but you could see one at any time and in any place. You will never see one if you spend all your time pounding the pillow back in camp. The open season is short and highly antici-pated throughout North America, and it ends far too soon. Go, hunt, suffer the elements; get the job done. I have shot deer in the first moments of opening day and I have taken them in the final min-utes of legal daylight on the last day of the season. You can do everything right all season long but you still cannot predict where and when a whitetail will finally appear. I can guarantee one thing: It will not happen if you are not out there. I can also guarantee that someone (maybe even me!) will shoot your deer for you if you aren't in the woods where you belong. I have done it many time in many states, and feel not the least bit of regret for the guy who elected to stay in bed rather than brave the frosty dawn one more time. In actual time lapsed it takes less than 20 seconds to see and shoot a deer, but it won't happen if you're not there.

1. RIFLES AND SHOTGUNS

Most rifle- and shotgun-hunting seasons open with a grand fusillade, and from the sounds of it you would think that tagging stations around the county would be inundated with freshly killed deer. Sadly, most of those projectiles go whistling into the distance, leaving hunters with little more than sad tales to tell at the end of the day, and in most cases the shooter alone is to blame.

I have seen the same phenomenon every season since I was old enough to hunt: It's Friday evening, the day before Opening Day, and sporting goods counters across the country are packed with anxious hunters looking for bargain rifles, shotguns and ammunition. I don't know how or why, but these hunters seem to think that if you buy a new gun at the store it is ready to go hunting straight out of the box. They don't fire one round through the gun to a) see if it works properly and b) hits where it is aimed. Even worse is when a hunter buys a new gun and a new scope, tightens down the screws and goes hunting. For some reason, these fellows think that a new gun and new scope are factory sighted and ready to go. In fact, such a gun may shoot three feet or more off the mark at 50 yards. That is enough to miss or mortally wound any large deer anywhere in North America.

Get Familiar with Your Firearm
Missing a deer is bad enough, but wounding and losing them should be unacceptable in any camp. Such unhappy circumstances can be avoided by

simply taking the time to properly set up and sight in a new (or long unused) rifle, shotgun or muzzle-loader. The process is easy and takes just a few minutes, but it can make all the difference in how your deer season goes.

Learning by doing is a common approach, but learning by knowing is more efficient. Doing things the wrong way can render an expensive gun or scope inoperable, void the warranty and ruin a hunt, so stop pretending that you know everything.

Learn what you need to know:
- Read the owner's manual that comes with your new firearm, especially information on loading and unloading and how the safety devices function.
- Familiarize yourself with the gun. Unfamiliarity with the firearm is a major cause of self-inflicted injuries.
- Read the manual for any scope or other sight you purchase for your gun.

Before you shoot any firearm:
- Make sure the action and barrel are clean, clear of dirt or obstructions.
- Look into the action and look down the barrel.
- Be sure all stock, barrel, sling, sight and scope screws are tight.

Making these adjustments after you shoot could affect the impact of your bullets or slugs, some-times with enough variation to cause a miss. With your firearm and sights tightened and secure, it's time to head to the range.

Rifle Sighting

I have shot deer in the cedar swamps of Maine, the vast prairies of Montana and the open oak woods of Georgia. For all these occasions I sighted my rifles in the same way. The key to success wherever you hunt is carefully sighting in your firearm — and knowing when not to shoot.

Most hunters consider themselves expert marksmen, good enough to hit a gnat in the eye at 1,000 yards, but the statistics prove otherwise. Most deer are shot at 100 yards or less, and most deer shot at beyond that distance are missed! It's not the gun's fault — a rifle is a machine meant to send a bullet downrange with accuracy and consistency.

As with any machine, it's the operator who is most often at fault when things go wrong. You can generally avoid missing your target at any reasonable range (out to about 250 yards) if you properly sight in, and you can avoid lost or wounded game if you can recognize when you are unable to hold your sights steady enough to make an effective shot, regardless of the distance.

- Plan to shoot from a steady rest. Sand bags are great, a rolled-up jacket will do but a commercial bench rest is best of all. Most commercial, state or club shooting ranges have solid benches to shoot from, measured target lanes and wood or metal frames that serve as permanent target holders.

Before you sight in:
- Always ensure that the backstop is safe, solid

and properly maintained. No bullets should be able to fly past the backstop.

- Remove bottles, cans, rocks or other debris that may cause a ricochet. Good places to shoot are at a premium these days. When using these or other facilities, keep them clean and support them with a donation!
- Pick a clear, calm morning or afternoon to do your shooting.
- Use targets you can clearly see.
- Bring along binoculars or a spotting scope so you can see where your bullets are hitting.

Set your first target at 25 yards (I'll explain why after your first three-shot string). Set up your sand bags or rest and settle in, gun unloaded with the action open, and just look through the scope or sights. Wiggle the rifle around until the sights or crosshairs sit solidly on the center of the bull's-eye with little or no effort. At this point we simply want to be sure we can get a good, tight grouping of shots somewhere in the target at this distance.

Sighting Shots

Be sure the range is clear of other shooters and spectators, and then prepare to shoot.

- Settle in and fire three carefully aimed shots at the center of the bull's-eye.
- Aim and shoot the same way each time no matter where the bullets are going. You are not trying to hit the bull's-eye this time: you're just looking for a nice, tight grouping of shots.

If you've done things properly thus far you'll have three holes in the paper — somewhere — very close together. Excellent!

Adjust Your Sights

Adjust your sights or scope according to the owner's manual.

In general, scope sights are moved left or right, up or down in the direction you want the bullet to go. The same goes for the rear sight if you are using V-notch, peep or other iron sights.

- Don't overdo your sight adjustments; in most cases a "click" equals an inch at 100 yards – a lot of adjustment if your bullets are only one-half inch off the mark.
- After you've made your adjustments, wait a few moments for the rifle barrel to cool down. If you can't touch it, it's too hot to shoot. Waiting till the barrel is stone cold may be impractical and is unnecessary, but, the cooler the barrel the more honest the grouping, because your first shots at a deer will be most likely to exit from a cold barrel.
- When you are ready to shoot again, continue aiming dead center and fire three more shots. These bullets should land closer to the bull's-eye, if not in the bull's-eye.
- Continue the sighting process until you have three closely centered holes in the center of the bull's-eye.

Why 25 Yards?

When sighted in at 25 yards, any modern center-fire rifle in the .24- .30-caliber range will be:

- Dead on at 25 yards
- Three inches high at 100
- Dead on again at approximately 250 yards.

Of course, calibers, loads and conditions will vary so your rifle may be off an inch or two beyond 25 yards,

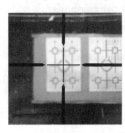

but a rifle so sighted will allow you to confidently shoot at deer out to 250 yards and expect to make a killing shot. All things being equal, your rifle will kill 99 percent of the deer you see in North America if you sight it in to be dead on at 25 yards.

SHOTGUNS AND MUZZLELOADERS

Range and Accuracy

In general, it is best to sight in shotguns and muzzleloaders to be slightly high at 25 yards, a few inches high at 50 yards and dead on at 100 yards. The issue is not that such guns can't kill deer at longer ranges. The problem is that large, slow projectiles fly in rainbow-like arcs that make it difficult to hit deer-sized targets much beyond these distances. It is possible to kill at deer at 125 yards with today's specially-manufactured sabot-slug guns and muzzleloaders, but accuracy and energy drop exponentially beyond 125 yards. Mathematically, of course, it can be done, but practically speaking, you're asking for trouble, most often in the form of wounded game.

Modern sabot-slug shotguns are dependable out to a maximum range of about 125 yards, and some state-of-the-art muzzleloaders are capable of pie-plate accuracy (able to keep all hits within an 8-inch circle) at 200 yards and more. With practice and diligence an accomplished shooter can improve on these numbers, but unless you are the exception, err on the side of caution and keep your shots at deer under 100 yards whenever possible.

Rather than philosophize about the extremes of firearm potential (some blackpowder arms are deadly out to 500 yards and more, though it would be irresponsible to attempt such shots at live game under normal hunting conditions), let's say for the sake of success that you should not attempt shots at deer beyond 250 yards with a modern centerfire rifle, 150 yards with an in-line muzzleloader or 100 yards with a slug gun. Yes, it can be done, but the risks are too high. If you push the envelope and attempt risky shots at long range, the odds are that you are going to start wounding and losing deer. This is irresponsible and unsportsmanlike. If you can't call your shot (state with confidence that you will place your projectile into a deer's heart-lung area) the responsible thing to do is move closer or pass up the shot.

Sighting at Various Distances
To know with certainty where your particular firearm places its bullets at various distances:

- Fire three-shot groups at close, medium and long range just to see where the projectiles hit.
- You will not be far off the mark with most "deer caliber" rifles, but don't be surprised if your shots start to roam at the longer distances. It's not the gun's fault! A rifle with tight sights, proper ammunition and a cold barrel will shoot far better than you can hold it. Admit your limitations as well as those of your fireaarm. Never exceed them!
- At long range, an errant breath of wind, a jiggle or twitch on your part, even a heartbeat, can send a bullet to the edge of the paper at 200 yards. Don't blame the gun. Learn from this.
- Know when a deer is too far for you to accurately shoot, and either find a way to get closer or abort the shot.
- If you know you can't hold your sights tightly and steadily on target, do not shoot.

Once your firearm is sighted in, coddle the gun for the duration of the season.

- Carry it in a padded case.
- Do not let anyone handle the gun, fool with the sights or play with your ammunition.
- Do not transport a scoped rifle or shotgun in a window firearm rack – the incessant pounding of highway miles will eventually

knock the scope off zero.
- If you suspect that your firearm has been dropped or tampered with, go through the sighting-in process again, starting with tightening the stock and sight screws.

Practice, Practice, Practice!

Familiarity with your firearm of choice is the first step in delivering a clean, killing shot when the time comes. To be consistently good shots, hunters must practice not only at the range, but also in situations similar to the hunting conditions they expect to encounter in the field. I routinely shoot 1,000 or more rounds out of my pellet rifle on basement targets during the summer, and as soon as squirrel season opens I pursue bushy-tails with a .22 till deer season opens. I spend many days at the range practicing at varying distances with a variety of rifles, sights and calibers.

After all those months of precision rifle shooting at small targets, finding a deer in my scope is like shooting at a moose at 10 yards! I am always amazed at how big a deer's shoulder looks in my scope, and it's almost too easy to place the crosshairs on the heart-lung area and make a clean, killing shot at normal woods distances.

2. MARKSMANSHIP

If there is one constant that every deer hunter should remember, it's "take a rest." No shooting position other than prone offers the stability of a solid rest. In most cases deer will give you the few seconds you need to rest your rifle against a rock, a tree or a log and get that steady, solid sight picture that's required to make a killing shot at any reasonable distance.

Whenever possible, spend time at the range or in the back yard practicing the various shooting positions (prone, sitting, kneeling and offhand) using your favorite deer rifle, a .22 or even a pellet rifle or BB gun. Hunting is not a perfect science and many things can happen in the blink of an eye – deer are unpredictable in spite of our best efforts to outwit them! You may be a dead shot from the prone position, but what if you're kneeling down examining tracks and your buck appears, or you are sitting in a ground blind and your trophy comes, not from in front where you expected it, but directly behind you? Will you be able to make the shot? In most cases, the answer is "No" because the hunter did not take the time to practice making difficult shots from unfamiliar positions.

The opportunity doesn't come up very often, but being able to shoot left-handed or right-handed can make or break a hunt. Doing so requires some forethought and planning, but it's a plus to be able to shoot equally well from either side.

Where to Hit Them

There are many places a bullet can be sent that will kill a deer, and armchair experts love to pontificate about the oddities, the rarities and the miraculous, but that is not a good route for the average hunter. Certainly a brain, spine or neck shot will kill a deer, but if you are not able to consistently place your bullet inside a 2-inch circle at a given range, why chance it?

I learned my lesson on "trick shooting" one fall when I was creeping through some thick brush and had stopped for a moment to look and listen. Almost immediately I heard the distinct sound of a deer walking in the leaves ahead of me, and

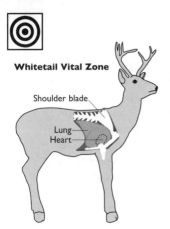

Whitetail Vital Zone

Shoulder blade

Lung
Heart

just then a nice, fat buck walked into view less than 15 yards away. Suddenly, the buck began to rub his antlers on a thick sapling! The wind was right, I was obscured by brush — the deer had no idea I was there. I watched in my scope as he rubbed, moving his head up and down erratically and jerkily like a man trying to whittle a very dry, knotty stick. I realized that the only shot I'd have would be his head – the rest of him was swallowed up in brush. I figured that I could not miss at such short range, and simply held my crosshairs on the base of his ear and waited for him to hesitate a moment, giving me the shot I wanted.

After several anxious seconds my chance came and I fired. In that instant the buck raised his head to rub farther up the sapling, and my bullet, a 180-grain .30-06 slug, struck him, not behind the ear as planned, but about two inches low, right on the point of the jawbone! The buck dropped like a stone, but was instantly up and thrashing around me, bouncing around like a rabbit hit by a car. He was obviously mortally wounded, with most of the far side of his face missing, but I had to shoot him again, this time behind the ear as I'd originally planned, to put him down for good.

The damage my bullet had inflicted was horrendous. The little buck was so disfigured by the shot that I could not even pose with him for photos. Sure, no meat was ruined in the process, but I found the entire episode distasteful and vowed then and there to never chance that kind of shot again.

The one good, sensible "money shot" on a deer is halfway up behind the shoulder – the old, reliable heart-lung shot.

A deer-caliber bullet placed here will kill any whitetail or muley it hits within a few yards. There will be plenty of blood sign for tracking and, in most cases, the deer will be found dead within 100 yards with no follow-up shot required.

The advantages of waiting for a clean, broadside shot far outweigh the risks involved in aiming for the brain, spine or neck.

At best, you'll miss, and at worst, the deer will run off and create a tracking situation that, compounded by confounding conditions (snow, rain or extremely dry weather, darkness or property disputes) could end in a lost deer that will suffer and die later.

It is not enough to hit a deer, wound it or otherwise count coup on the animal.

There is never an "at least I hit it" scenario that is acceptable to the sport. Reckless shooting, taking chance shots at iffy targets or shooting at running deer should not be allowed. The big talkers will go on about their prowess as great game shots, but the fact is that few hunters are capable of making any and all shots presented to them.

- It is not acceptable to risk the life of an animal based on luck or fervent wishes. Know your own limitations and have the maturity to pass up uncertain shots if you know you can't make them.
- Remember — most modern deer-caliber rifles are capable of hitting an 8-inch circle at 250 yards. If you've sighted your rifle in to hit dead on at 25 yards you can kill any deer you see under woods conditions.
- Wait — let the deer move about as it wishes.
- Wait for the standing, broadside shot and, if necessary, let the deer move 25, 50 or even 100 yards farther out. You can put that bullet where it needs to go, so keep calm, aim straight and wait for the best opportunity.

WHEN NOT TO SHOOT

Look Beyond the Target

- Never shoot at deer where you can see other hunters nearby, orange clothing in the distance, houses, vehicles or other obstacles that may or may not be occupied or operated by humans.
- Do not shoot at deer moving along a sky-line unless you know what's behind the deer (Woods? a swamp? a farmhouse? a school?).
- Avoid shooting at running deer for two reasons – you probably won't make a killing shot and you can't keep track of your sights, the deer, his line of travel and what's around him

to the safety of everyone concerned. A deer can cover 100 yards in a few seconds, changing his backdrop, line of angle and elevation just enough to put distant people, vehicles or buildings in jeopardy. As our ballistics tables tell us, a bullet from the average deer rifle can cover 2,500 feet in one second – that's about one-half mile! Unless you know everything about what's inside that half-mile crescent in front of you, do not shoot!

There are other situations when you should refrain from taking a shot — when deer are:

- Swimming (illegal in most areas)
- Crossing roads
- Running back through a line of drivers
- Moving through urban areas where homes lights and vehicles can be seen in the distance
- When you are not sure whether it is a buck, doe or fawn

The proper thing to do when confronted with uncertain situations is *nothing!* Let the deer go, or wait for a better shot. Never shoot at uncertain targets; the cost of impatience is simply too high!

3. SAFETY MUST COME FIRST!

Imagine the excitement of hearing the crunch of frosty leaves at first light, that adrenalin-rushing gleam of antlers in the pre-dawn, the hulking form of a monster buck through the brush exactly where you expected him to appear. You take careful aim, flip off the safety and, with practiced confidence, squeeze the trigger. At the boom of the shot your target drops to the ground, and with heart-pounding elation you walk over to find — your father, your brother or your best friend lying in a pool of blood, a gaping hole in his chest — dead!

This year, and every year, a hunter in every state will find himself in this situation, killing or severely wounding another human who was "mistaken for game." The aftermath is traumatic, to say the least. Very few of the hunters who have injured or killed another human while hunting have ever gone back to the sport. Their momentary lapse in judgment ruined hunting for them, their families, the victim and his family. Most states require new hunters to complete a hunter safety course before a license will be issued, and the majority of states now require the wearing of fluorescent orange clothing while hunting during firearms seasons. Even so, hunters are being shot every year, and those accidents, while diminishing as time goes on, can be avoided.

The rules have always been simple ones:

- Never shoot at a target you have not positively identified.
- Never shoot at noises in the brush; never shoot randomly into woods where a deer was seen (even moments before).
- Never shoot at "brown," even if you think it has to be a deer.

POSITIVELY IDENTIFY YOUR TARGET – IT'S THE ONLY WAY TO BE CERTAIN AND SAFE!

PROTECT YOURSELF!

Much is made of being certain of your target while shooting, but many accidents these days involve self-inflicted wounds primarily due to careless, unsafe handling of firearms. Every firearm has one or more safety devices installed, but as any hunter safety course instructor will tell you, those are machined parts, and machined parts can and will fail. Never trust a safety or lock when your life is at stake!

The rules of safe gun handling always apply, even when you are alone.

- When you carry your rifle or shotgun, be sure both hands are on it, be sure the safety is on and be sure the muzzle is pointed in a safe direction at all times.
- If you must put the firearm down for any reason (while resting, crossing streams or fences, or while field dressing game) unload the chamber and leave the action open!
- Never lean a loaded firearm against a rock, log, tree, building or vehicle.
- Never place a loaded firearm in or on a vehicle, case or gun rack; and never handle a firearm by the barrel or muzzle.

Do not allow your companions to handle their firearms carelessly, either. Nothing is more frightening than looking down the muzzle of a firearm you know, or think, may be loaded – the possibility of an accidental discharge is real for a variety of reasons and, as the saying goes, you get only one mistake. Guns that are dropped, bumped, tossed or tripped over are the ones that "accidentally" kill, and every such incident can be avoided if all hunters practiced basic safety skills and adhered to the NRA's Ten Commandments of Gun Safety. Post these simple rules in your hunting camp, tent or den and refer to them every time you head out the door for a day in the woods. One day you or someone you know will be glad you did!

NRA's Ten Commandments of Gun Safety

I.   Watch that muzzle. Control it's direction at all times.

II. Treat every firearm with the respect due a loaded firearm.

III. Be sure of your target and beyond before you pull the trigger. Know the identifying features of the game you hunt.

IV. Be sure the barrel and action are clear of obstructions. Carry only ammunition of the proper size for the firearm you are using.

V.   Unload firearms when not in use. Leave the action open. Firearms should be carried empty in cases to and from shooting areas.

VI. Point a firearm only at something you want to shoot.

VII. Unload a firearm before you carry it while climbing a fence or tree or jumping a ditch. Pull a firearm toward you by the butt, not the muzzle.

VIII. Shoot bullets only when you have an adequate backstop. Do not shoot at a hard, flat surface or water.

IX. Store firearms and ammunition in secured locations beyond the reach of children or careless adults.

X.   Avoid alcoholic beverages or other mood-altering drugs before and during shooting.

4. BALLISTICS

To better understand what happens to your bullet as it flies downrange to the target, it's important to have a basic understanding of ballistics. Though no one has ever said so, most hunters start out believing that a bullet travels in a straight line indefinitely, and the only reason we miss is because we didn't "aim straight." This is not the case, as we shall see.

A bullet actually begins to fall the instant it leaves the muzzle of the barrel. The forces of speed, gravity, climate, wind and rotation begin to act on the projectile immediately. Some bullets (notably the heavier, slower slugs in the .40 calibers and up) will drop faster, while the smaller, lighter bullets will drop at a slower rate and therefore be "more accurate" out to longer ranges. A .458 Winchester Magnum bullet, for example, is heavy and slow, and will drop precipitously as a result, while a centerfire .22-caliber slug will drop almost inconspicuously by comparison. Truth be told, a .458 bullet can be made to hit a long-range target by simply adjusting the sights to account for the nearly 6-foot drop below the line of sight at 400 yards, but this is nothing the average deer hunter will want to be concerned with.

What hunters do need to know is that, for most "deer calibers," meaning rifles in the .24- to .35 caliber range, a rifle sighted in to hit dead on at 25 yards will be approximately three inches high at 100 yards, dead on at 200 yards and four to six inches low at 250 yards. This, in deer-hunter's parlance, is "suitable" accuracy for big game when shooting from a rest at a fully exposed, standing deer at any distance out to a known 250 yards.

It is likely that you will hunt your entire life and never get an opportunity to shoot at a standing deer at 250 yards, but if you've done your homework (tight sight and stock screws, careful sighting-in at the range, solid rest) you can reasonably expect to hit what you aim at and to recover the animal as a result.

The following is a table showing the velocity of many popular deer cartridges, the energy in foot-pounds (at the muzzle), and the trajectory, or arc, of the fired bullet out to 200 yards. While there are many variables in calculating bullet performance on game including bullet design (its lead core makeup, metal jacket, point or tip configuration, speed and rotation), we'll leave the engineering discourse for more detailed books on the subject. For the stated purpose of being able to kill a deer with one shot with minimal meat damage and little follow-up tracking required, let's say that the listed cartridges are the ones recommended for deer under most circumstances and conditions in North America. Not every one is ideal for every situation (there is no such gun) but with a little forethought, practice, knowledge and ability, any one of these selected cartridges will down any whitetail or mule deer you will encounter in America, Canada or Alaska. In other words, do your job and the bullet will perform as it was designed.

COMMON DEER RIFLE BALLISTICS

Caliber	Bullet	Velocity	Energy	Trajectory (yards)		
				100	200	300
.243 Win.	100 Grain	2960	1950	1.6	0	-7.1
6mm	100 Grain	3100	2121	1.1	0	-6.7
.270 Win.	140 Grain	3100	2990	1.4	0	-7.3
7mm-08	140 Grain	2860	2542	2	0	7.6
7mm Mag.	160 Grain	2950	3090	1.5	0	-7.9
.30/30	170 Grain	2200	1827	0	-8.2	-30
.300 Savage	150 Grain	2630	2305	2.4	0	-10.4
.308 Win.	165 Grain	2700	2670	2.2	0	-8.4
.30/06	180 Grain	2700	2915	2	0	11
.300 Mag.	180 Grain	2960	3500	1.5	0	-6.6
.338 Mag.	250 Grain	2650	3899	2.1	0	8.5
.35 Rem.	200 Grain	2020	1812	0	-12.1	-43.9
.444 Marlin	240 Grain	2350	2942	0	-18.1	-65.1
.45/70	300 Grain	1810	2182	0	-13.8	-50.1

SHOTGUN SLUG BALLISTICS - 12 Gauge Slugs

Load	Slug	Energy/Trajectory (yards)				
		Muzzle	25	50	75	100
Federal Prem. rifled	Foster (1 oz.)	1645/ 0	1390/ 0.5	1205/ 0	1070/ -2.3	965/ -6.5
Remington Slugger HV	Foster (0.875 oz.)	2989/ 0	2180/ -0.2	1442/ 0	1121/ -2.3	847/ -7.4
Winchester Super-X rifled	Foster (1 oz.)	2488/ 0	2056/ 0.4	1310/ 0	768/ -1.9	953/ -5.9

SHOTGUN SLUG BALLISTICS - Full Bore Loads

Load	Slug	Energy/Trajectory (yards)				
		Muzzle	25	50	75	100
Brenneke	Heavy Field Mag. (1 oz.)	2538/ 0	2000/ 1.8	1601/ 2.9	1346/ 2.4	1170/ 0
Rottweil	Brenneke MP (1 oz.)	2215/ 0	1640/ 0.1	1250/ 0	1025/ -2	890/ -5.4

SHOTGUN SLUG BALLISTICS - 12 Gauge Sabots

Load	Slug	Energy/Trajectory (yards)				
		Muzzle	25	50	75	100
Federal	Barnes Ex (1 oz.)	2260/0	2055/1.3	1870/2	1710/1.6	1560/0
Winchester	BRI (1 oz.)	1821/-0.9	1678/0.3	1259/0	1101/-2	975/-6
Lightfield	Commander (1.25 oz.)	3274/0	2712/2.7	2241/1.23	1856/1.21	1355/0

BUCKSHOT

Load	Charge	Energy					
		Muzzle	20	30	40	50	60
Remington Express 000	(10 pellets)	230	180	161	145	131	119
Rem. Exp. 00	(9 pellets)	212	159	139	123	110	98
Federal Prem. 000	(10 pellets)	230	180	161	145	131	119
Federal Premium 00	(12 pellets)	202	152	134	119	106	87
Winchester SuperX 00	(9 pellets)	212	159	139	123	110	98
Winchester SuperX 0	(12 pellets)	177	133	117	103	92	83

BLACK POWDER LOADS

Bullet	Type	Charge	Muzzle Velocity	Muzzle Energy
.45 cal.	128 gr. Round Ball	70 gr. FFFg	1950	1080
	240 gr. Maxi-Ball	90 gr. FFFg	1659	1466
	158 gr. Sabot	80 gr. FFg	1840	1186
.50 cal.	178 gr. Round Ball	90 gr. FFg	1950	1502
	370 gr. Maxi-Ball	100 gr. FFg	1418	1648
	250 gr. Sabot	100 gr. FFg	1625	1462
.54 cal.	230 gr. Round Ball	100 gr. FFg	1855	1758
	430 gr. Maxi-Ball	110 gr. FFg	1428	1948
	300 gr. Sabot	110 gr. FFg	1578	1656

PYRODEX LOADS

Bullet	Type	Charge	Muzzle Velocity	Muzzle Energy
.45 cal	150 gr. Sabot	80 gr. RS/Sel	1920	1227
	200 gr. Sabot	100 gr. P	2075	1910
	285 gr. Buffalo Bullet	100 gr. RS/Sel.	1458	1339
.50 cal.	200 gr. Sabot	100 gr. RS/Sel.	1810	1454
	250 gr. Sabot	100 gr. P	1730	1660
	370 gr. Maxi-Ball	100 gr. RS/Sel.	1525	1905
.54 cal.	260 gr. Sabot	100 gr. RD/Sel.	1620	1513
	425 gr. Buffalo Bullet	120 gr. RS/Sel.	1536	2222

PYRODEX PELLET LOADS

Bullet	Type	Charge (Pellets)	Muzzle Velocity	Muzzle Energy
.45 cal.	150 gr. Sabot	(2) 50 gr./.45 cal.	2225	1650
	200 gr. Sabot	(3) 50 gr./.45 cal.	2247	2240
.50 cal.	240 gr. Sabot	(2) 50 gr./.50 cal.	1730	1593
	250 gr. Sabot	(3) 50 gr./.50 cal.	1975	2162
	350 gr. Maxi-Hunter	(2) 50 gr./.50 cal.	1518	1792
.54 cal	300 gr. Sabot	(2) 60 gr./.54 cal.	1701	1923
	430 gr. Conical	(2) 60 gr./.54 cal.	1425	1935

5. DEER BEHAVIOR, HABITS AND HABITAT

Deer have been studied and observed for well over 200 years in North America, and hundreds of books have been written about their behavior, yet hunter success rates remain remarkably low. Everything pertaining to deer and their habitat has been examined and reviewed by scientists, writers and hunters, and yet, in a normal confrontation between deer and hunter, the deer is most likely to win.

Because we don't know what makes deer react to certain stimuli, or how they'll react under specific circumstances, there is never going to be a time when all hunters who enter the woods will fill their tags. Events occur that are uncontrollable and unpredictable, but the one common thread in all successful deer hunts is that the hunter was in the right place at the right time. Things can go entirely wrong and still the hunter can succeed. For example, in Massachusetts a 17-year-old girl plagued by a broken hip hobbled into the woods one afternoon, decided she was in the wrong place and moved 20 feet, directly into the path of an oncoming buck. She fired twice at the buck and missed. Her shotgun jammed and she fired again — and missed! She cleared the action and calmly loaded the chamber with her fourth and last slug. She took careful aim at the deer, which stood still and watched her the entire time, and finally downed what was to be the biggest whitetail taken in the state that year — a 190-class nontypical the likes of which few hunters ever see!

Luck has much to do with successful deer hunting, but only to a point. To put the odds in your favor more often, there are some basic things the hunter should know about deer and how they act during the hunting season.

Food

Deer are herbivorous animals, meaning they eat plants (grasses, leaves and soft, woody material) and they are browsers, which means they spend

much of their active time nipping bits of greenery here and there from various plants as they walk along. Most of this activity takes place at night, but deer can be seen feeding during the day, especially late in the fall and winter when food becomes scarce and they must invest more "time per pound" to fill their stomachs. A deer will consume approximately two quarts of food per day, which may not sound like much, but if you were to try to fill a two-quart container with grass, twigs and leaves at a deer's hesitant, cautious pace, you'd see that the process could require several hours, and those are the hours in which a deer is most vulnerable to predation and hunting.

In most areas deer will take advantage of a variety of food:

- Pasture grasses
- Palatable twigs (maple, apple, greenbrier, etc.)
- Agricultural crops — apples, corn, oats, soybeans (and the weeds that grow among them), rye, wheat, etc.
- Ornamental shrubs and many decorative flowers and shrubs (this is why deer are so numerous in agricultural and suburban areas). Variety is the key. A good mix of grasslands, forest (for mast production including acorns, beechnuts and similar natural foods), brushy cover and water will attract and hold deer for as long as the cover remains mixed. Areas with little or no variety in cover types (open fields, climax woodlands — such as our national forests and state forests — and plots of unsavory crops such as cotton, tobacco and potatoes) will attract and hold few deer.

In general, if the cover is open, airy and convenient for hunters to penetrate, there will be few deer in evidence. When the cover is deemed "too thick" for good hunting, that's where you want to place your stand!

Water

Some hunters believe that deer never drink water, that they get all the moisture they need from the plants they eat, but the truth is that deer simply

adapt to what is available to them. In wetland areas, deer will drink water from time to time, though hunting over "water holes" specifically to ambush deer coming in to drink, is probably not a good strategy. Deer drink quickly and sporadically when they do partake of water, and hunters will rarely see them do so. In arid regions, deer may live out their entire lives without taking a single gulp of water, yet they can survive and thrive on the moisture contained in the plants they eat.

From a hunting standpoint, the benefit of water is that wetlands produce grass and brush, and this means forage and cover for deer. Lakeshore cover, stream and river corridors and marshy swamplands are ideal places to look for deer. Not only do these areas provide more succulent foods for deer, but the presence of water creates obstacles that force deer to travel or cross in certain places, which can aid the hunter in deciding where to place a stand or still-hunt.

Also, water can be considered a hunter's highway. In many areas, hunting by canoe or johnboat along lake shores or river channels can put hunters into some good, remote areas where few other hunters will be found. Deer seem to be less fearful of hunters approaching in a watercraft, and scouting via boat or canoe can reveal major crossings, bedding or feeding areas that may never have been hunted.

Scent

One of the great mysteries in hunting deer is that of scent. What, when and how do they interpret what they smell? One whiff of the wrong odor can send a herd of deer bounding away, and you will not see those deer again! We can't expect to fully understand scent as it applies to deer, but we do know that it must be taken seriously if you want to shoot more deer during your hunting career!

Scent is important to deer because it's how they identify each other, detect danger and find food. All things bring scent to a deer's attention – the ground, the vegetation and the wind catch, hold and deliver scent particles to the animal's nose, and from there the mystery begins. Sometimes a deer will react violently to a sudden whiff of human scent, bounding wildly away snorting and whistling in a panic. Other times a deer will ignore fresh human scent. In fact, most deer now live close enough to humans, homes and highways that "unnatural" scents must assail their nostrils constantly. We will probably never know what scents will alert a deer to danger or what their reaction will be in every case.

The important thing for the hunter to know is that human-based scents (food, tobacco, alcohol, oil, gasoline, coffee and body odor) are not common in a deer's world. On their own, these may not send a deer galloping through the woods in a panic, but they will alert a deer to your presence, and that is what I call "strike one." Now you have one of the most alert game animals on

earth focused on "something" that is not quite right in its environment. An errant breeze has told the deer to stop what it's doing, pay attention and find out where that smell is coming from.

Now you will have eyes and ears on you as well, and if the deer smells and sees you, or smells and hears you, that's "strike two," and he will generally react in any number of self-preserving ways, most likely by bounding out of sight, often before you even know he's there.

Hunters do many things to hide or mask their odors:

- Carefully wash hunting clothes separately using special scent-free soaps, bag them in scent-free plastic bags. (Some hunterrs choose to carry the bag into the woods and put the clothes on near their hunting site).
- Hang hunting coats in bags filled with locally-cut boughs — pine, cedar or oak — so that the coat will take on the "natural" scent of the local foliage.

- Climb high into tree stands and hope that the elevated scent won't be carried to the deer moving about down below.
- Use high-tech (usually activated charcoal impregnated) commercial scent-block hunting clothing.

Because deer can walk into a snow-covered cornfield in January, paw down into two feet of snow and find a half-cob of corn that the picker had missed two months before, it may be silly for us to think we can beat a deer's sense of smell with manufactured bags, scent blockers and such.

NOTE: Sooner or later a deer approaching your stand or blind is going to smell you or see you.

We can't know what a deer senses in a given situation; all we can do is be ready and make a good, killing shot when the opportunity arises.

REMEMBER: The key to successful deer hunting is to be alert on stand, pay attention to the small sounds and sights of the woods and be ready to shoot the instant a deer appears.

THE RUT

One of the best things to happen to deer hunters is "the rut," that period in late fall when female deer are ready to breed and the bucks are more than willing to accommodate them. Deer may be encountered at any time throughout the season, but this is the one time of year when trophy-class bucks, the mature trophies few hunters ever see alive in the woods, are most vulnerable. Normally reclusive and nocturnal, big bucks essentially lose their knack for self-preservation as they exhaust themselves in pursuit of receptive females.

Bucks that would normally be bedded in secluded, thickets throughout the day will be found running wild-eyed through the open woods at high noon. They will travel many miles away from their home range as they seek does to breed, and this reckless behavior, while good for ensuring the future of the herd, is the reason why so many trophy deer mounts adorn the walls of hunters throughout North America.

In general, the period from late October through mid-November is the "peak" of the rut in North America. Peak dates vary from region to region, but if you can arrange to be in the woods somewhere between Oct. 25 and Nov. 20, you can expect to enjoy some of the best hunting of your life.

Does will be more active as they feed heavily in anticipation of the coming winter, and the bucks will be pushing and prodding does night and day as the urge to breed overwhelms them.

There are various phases of the rut (as characterized by humans):
- Pre-rut, the chase phase
- Mating
- Post-rut

For hunters looking for venison or a trophy, the bottom line is to be out there during the rut!

Anything can happen at any time and most likely what does occur will involve does and bucks participating in some phase of the rut.

The nighttime activities of deer, though fascinating and interesting, are of little concern to sportsmen, who are not allowed to hunt or shoot deer during the hours of darkness. In fact, it often confounds hunters who drive around at night and see herds of deer in roadside fields, yet at dawn there's no sign of them. Deer will bed down in fields at night, often in plain sight of roads and houses, but by daylight they will be far back in the woods, especially when the leaf cover is gone and daytime visibility is high.

Bucks will be active throughout the day, so hunters should plan their rut-period trips so they can spend as much time as possible in areas where does are numerous and active. Those traveling bucks are not looking for food, they're looking for does to breed.

This normally means hunting feeding areas or travel routes to the deer's daytime bedding zones. (It is best not to disturb deer in their bedding areas because if they are pushed out too many times they will seek other, even more secluded areas for daytime security.) Good places to set up for rutting deer include the brushy edges, borders and hedgerows of farm fields, clear-cuts, waterway borders and mast-producing forest (oak and beech especially).

Does will be found feeding and bedding in these areas and the bucks will be right behind them.

Also, when hunting such areas, plan to stay in the woods all day. Rutting bucks may travel many miles in search of does and may not find the trail of an estrous doe until hours after she has passed. Don't think that because some does passed your stand at dawn that the buck won't find them. It may be noon or even later, but eventually a rutting buck will encounter the scent of the does and begin looking for them. Stay put, be ready and reap your reward!

SEASONAL BEHAVIOR

Deer act significantly different in early fall than they do in late winter. The vagaries of climate, leaf cover and food availability all have something to do with why deer seem to be everywhere in September and nowhere in January.

Escape cover is always important to deer, and often determines how far a deer will run before stopping for a look back. In late summer the thick leaves on low-growing brush provide plenty of camouflage for deer. In fact, deer seen during the early archery seasons (late September and early October) seem almost relaxed. There is plenty to eat and cover galore.

As leafy cover dwindles and the woods become more open, deer sightings become less frequent during daylight until winter when, with no leaf cover, little food and harsh weather, the animals barely move at all, even when there is no snow on the ground. They simply can't afford the risk or the loss of calories.

Early Fall

In early fall deer are more active and far less stressed than in November, December or January. Bucks will travel together with does and fawns, and large groups of deer will be seen feeding placidly in open fields well into September and October.

As November approaches, the deer begin a shift in activity. Bucks produce rubs — saplings and small trees stripped bare of bark by the buck's antlers in the process of creat-

ing scent markings to announce their presence. They will also create scrapes, bare patches of ground marked by the scent glands in their feet.

Bucks separate and begin to spar with each other in more serious territorial battles, while the does and fawns spend their time feeding and bedding, and spend less time in the open during daylight hours.

November

This is when rutting activity nears its peak. Bucks will begin fighting seriously, often locking horns and even killing each other in major battles over territorial breeding rights. Dominant bucks will begin chasing does in earnest, spending long hours tending estrous does, breeding them and moving on immediately to find more receptive females. Bucks cover a lot of ground during the rut, and this exposes them to more hunters than at any other time of year.

This is the period when hunters should spend the maximum amount of time in the woods. The odds of encountering a rutting buck will never be higher, but you won't see him if you're not there! Plan to be in the woods before dawn and stay put till closing time (one-half hour after sunset in most states). You may see a buck at any time of the day, so bring a lunch, water and, if necessary, a good book to read (like this one!) to help you stay focused, alert and ready for your opportunity.

Winter

Many states allow deer hunting through January, and these are tough times for deer and for hunters. It's cold, there's no leaf cover, natural foods are gone and the deer are inactive for most of the day as they try to conserve their body fat. It's a tough time to be hunting because it's normally colder, windier and there is much less deer activity, but there are still plenty of chances to find deer, especially early in the morning and late in the evening as deer move to and from their bedding areas in search of food.

Bucks will still breed any does missed during the peak of the rut, but late-season breeding is minimal. The key now is to focus on feeding and bedding areas, places where more deer will spend most of their daylight hours. In general, this means thick cover, ideally brushy hollows, recent clear-cuts, swamps and other secluded areas where deer can bed and feed without wasting calories on unnecessary travel.

Dawn and dusk are the times to be in the woods as winter sets in. But, because late-season days are usually short (sunset is at 4:30 p.m. in some northern regions!), it's best to plan to spend the entire day in the woods.

Deer are never on a schedules like ours. Random events, noises or intrusions can make deer move about at any time of the day during any season. For hunters, the best advice is to spend the maximum amount of time in the woods and always expect the unexpected. Deer are creatures of habit, certainly, but they are also creatures of flight and fancy. We understand much about them but have yet to crack the secrets of why, when and what they will do next!

6. HUNTING LOCATIONS

Regardless of the phase of the rut, deer are creatures of thick brush and dense cover. They like to use hedgerows, forest edges and waterway borders to move between feeding and bedding areas. In general, if you can't see through it and it's too thick for hunters to move around in it without making a lot of noise, it's perfect for deer.

Some hunters are able to walk into unknown woods at dawn on opening day with no advance preparation and they will shoot a deer. It happens all the time. One hunter I know had one day to hunt and asked me about a good spot. I gave him some directions to a local wildlife management area I was familiar with and, later that week, he went there, walked in before daylight to a place he'd never seen, climbed into his tree stand and, by noon, had three deer on the ground! He might have shot more (the limit was five deer at the time and is now up to 12 deer!) but he ran out of arrows!

Now, I have hunted that same spot many times and have seen a few deer there, but this just illustrates the fact that luck has a lot to do with hunter success. In other words, don't be afraid to go with your gut feeling when it comes to picking a stand site. Any place can be "the place" when it comes to deer hunting. Your odds for success are higher if you go with what is known about deer behavior and habitat, but there is no reason you can't wander down the middle of an old woods trail at high noon swigging a cold soda, as happened to me when I shot my first deer!

That said, there are some odds-on choices the hunter can make when selecting places to hunt. The options are endless, of course, because deer will, over the course of their lifetime, utilize nearly every inch of their home territory. In good deer country, you can find tracks and other sign everywhere you look — in the woods, along the highway, beside the lake, on lawns, in gardens. Deer are mobile, curious and reactionary — a chance encounter with another hunter, a coyote or a dog will send them bounding for the hillsides, perhaps right into your lap!

Field Edges

In early fall, field edges are ideal places to find deer, especially in late afternoon. Many hunters pick a stand close to or within the thin brush within

sight of the open field or pasture, and often they will get a shot at deer that have entered the field. However, the better choice is to select a stand site inside the woods on trails approaching the field. The reason is that deer will come to the field from distant bedding areas and often linger in the shadows away from the field edge until nearly dark. If you're set up along a deer trail leading to the field and some distance away, you're more likely to see deer as they come to the field or pause nearby to wait for darkness to fall.

Most often, deer enter fall fields in low corners, high knolls or in low, swampy areas — wherever hunters are least likely to be because conditions, visibility or the wind favor the deer's approach. Expect them to come into a field slowly, tentatively and on high alert, does and fawns first, followed (sometimes!) by the bigger bucks.

In general, the best field stand sites are with the sun at your back and the wind in your face, but deer are not often fooled by conditions that favor the hunter. Their counterattack invariably includes coming into a field with the sun at their backs and the wind in their faces, so they can see or smell danger on the way into the open field. Deer have been dodging danger for thousands of years and they are very good at it!

The game, of course, is to pick the ideal spot so that you can see the area around you clearly yet the deer can come in without detecting your presence. Finding each field's "sweet spot" may take several trips, and in most cases you will make plenty of mistakes before you find out where the deer like to enter or leave a field using the surrounding brushy cover.

Hedgerows

The brushy strips of cover that separate fields from each other, border urban back yards or that surround creeks and ponds are ideal travel lanes for deer. In many areas of the Mid-West, for example, hedgerow hunting is the name of the game. Deer feed in the open crop fields, bed in big blocks of woods and travel to and from these areas via hedgerows and strips of brush and saplings.

Good stand sites include areas where:
- Woods and hedgerows meet
- Short breaks in the hedgerow cover (access roads, bar-ways and gates)
- Where the hedgerows narrow down to thin strips of cover near water, swamps and fallow land

There are invariably many well-used deer trails inside hedgerow cover, and these will give hunters some good ideas about where to place stands for specific situations. Wind is not so much of a concern here because the cover is thin and deer will not break from the protection of the brush unless serious danger threatens. If the wind is blowing directly down or up the hedgerow, the deer will have the advantage unless you can utilize a tree stand that puts you above the prevailing breezes.

Water Crossings

Water in any form (streams, rivers, lakes or ponds) surrounded by woods or brush offer ideal places to hunt for deer. Not only are these areas generally undeveloped, brushy and wooded, they are usually in areas where deer are naturally funneled to or around them by the topography of the land. There

is normally higher ground around water (because water generally lays or flows in the lowest areas of a region), and deer moving to and from the higher elevations will cross or skirt waterways in areas that are convenient to them.

Water crossings are easy to find. Simply hike along any brook or stream or skirt the edges of a lake or pond, and you will find deer tracks and trails that converge on the areas that are most convenient to cross – areas of low water, strips of thicker cover, peninsula bases or the like. In most cases, hunters will find that deer cross in the same places hunters would cross – deer are remarkably similar to us in their desire to make things easier on themselves!

Stand placement is simple enough when hunting such crossings. Build a blind or place a tree stand in such a way that the crossing or its approaches are in range, downwind and such that the sun will not be in your eyes at prime dawn and dusk hunting times.

Road Crossings

If you drive a car, you've seen "deer crossing" signs. These are probably the best indication of where deer can be found in any area because the number of car-deer accidents were so high in those areas that signs were placed to warn motorists. Because generation after generation of deer use the same natural crossings (until or unless the topography of the land is drastically altered by major airport, industrial park or subdivision construction), places where "deer crossing" signs are placed make excellent stand locations.

Of course, hunters should always seek landowner permission to hunt, install stands or build blinds, and this may not always be possible at every deer crossing in North America. However, such crossings exist by the thousands, wherever paved roads are found. Study a topographic map of the region, note the flow of the land, the things that make deer use these crossings (cover types, waterways, land elevations) and find a place that meets all of the hunter's requirements: Lots of deer activity, easy access, plenty of potential stand or blind locations.

The ideal road crossing is a narrow strip of cover or lowland topography that naturally funnels deer from one side of the road to the other, normally from woodlots to crop fields, pastures or other food sources. They may also consist of travel lanes deer use to avoid human activity or bypass open country. Scouting will reveal the heaviest travel lanes.

When a "deer crossing" seems to be nothing more than a wide, flat expanse of featureless country, such as the middle of a vast cornfield, swamp or other open area, simply examine a map or drive around the area till you find thick cover, topographic changes or other funneling sources where you can begin your quest for a stand site.

Keep in mind that some of the best road crossings can be the worst places to hunt from an aesthetic point of view. Forget the "wilderness" aspect of deer hunting – often, these crossings are near busy highways, roads or developments where human activity is loud and distracting. It is often the greater test of the hunter's mettle to remain focused and enthusiastic while vehicles, farm equipment, church bells and other annoyances clang and clamor throughout the day. However, such hunts are often worth the effort.

State Forests

Perhaps one of the most underutilized of all our public hunting grounds are our state forests. Most are managed for timber production, but these days wildlife management (which benefits deer and other game) is also included in forest management plans. Access is normally free and most forests are open to hunting under the general state rule (with some exceptions, which may be obtained from the state forest manager's office).

The key to hunting state forests is keeping track of the forest's timber management program. Most state forests are covered with climax-phase trees, those big, old "virgin" stands that tourists adore. However, there are also many miles of clear-cuts, those big, new stands of new growth that deer adore! Many of these timbering projects are tucked far back in the forest's holdings, rarely visible from nearby roads and practically unknown except to the loggers, haulers, foresters and hunters wise enough to ask where they are!

One clear-cut I discovered a few years ago produced a 10-point buck on my first trip and several smaller deer on subsequent expeditions. The clear-cut is essentially the entire back side of a mountain as it faces the road. You can't see it driving by, but if you park at the foot of the mountain by a gated road, walk about 30 minutes to the top and look over, the entire valley before you is one gigantic clear-cut and it is full of deer! In the 10 years I've successfully hunter there, I've never seen another hunter!

Cutting is conducted annually throughout these forests and in many cases access roads are gated, blocked off, or closed to motorized traffic. All of this means excellent opportunities for the hunter who has the energy and ambition to find and hunt these places.

Most state forests are clearly designated on maps. Local roads and trails are usually noted. For a clearer look, visit the state forest office and examine the official forest map. Ask the forester to point out clear-cut areas that are three to seven years old – these will be prime deer habitat this season. Thank the forester, study your maps, get in there and scout prior to the season and, as you're dragging your big buck out of the woods, be thankful there are such things as state forests!

Hunting Unfamiliar Areas

One of the greatest tools a hunter can have is a topographic map. Detailed maps of any area in North America are available online or through various mapping companies that allow hunters to pinpoint locations within a few feet utilizing any of the global positioning systems now on the market. Getting in and out is as easy as entering your present position and your destination. The GPS will do the rest!

When looking at topographic maps of potential hunting areas, elevations are the key. Find the places where deer can travel easiest such as mountain saddles, creek bottoms, river valleys and lake shorelines. Many times the "lay of the land" will dictate where deer will find the easiest traveling, and it's a simple matter of putting yourself there in time for a daylight or afternoon hunt.

In mountainous areas, peaks and valleys are good places to look for deer, as are saddles, plateaus and finger ridges, which deer use as travel lanes from higher ground into valley croplands or browsing areas.

No Substitute For Scouting

Probably the most used (and most ignored) word in deer hunting is "scouting." Apparently it sounds like work, takes too much time and confuses hunters who think "scouting" means you have to be a Jim Bridger or Daniel Boone to master the task. It's easier than you think! Scouting for deer is no different than what you do when you shop for cars, houses or furniture – guns and gear, too. You go, you look, you see what's out there, and you make your decision.

Perhaps the biggest mistake hunters make (especially the ones who complain that "there are no more deer") is failing to scout their hunting area or, after hunting the same place for a generation or more, failing to see that things have changed. If you have changed since you took your first deer at 13, be able to admit that those woods have changed, too. Sure, it's great to spend time hunting the same rock or tree where Grandpa shot his first deer, but take a good look around and tell yourself the truth – what in the world is a deer going to do today in all that open, mature forest? There's no food, no cover – no reason for a deer to be there! Deer may have been numerous during Grandpa's youth, but that was long ago. The brush is gone, the fields are gone – you're standing in a sterile environment where, through most of the day, you'll be lucky to see so much as a boreal songbird because wildlife diversity does not rhyme with climax forest!

Deer and other game are able to adapt to habitat changes. It's not that the deer are all dead – they simply moved to better conditions! Hunters must do the same, and scouting is simply a way of eliminating those sterile environments from your list of destinations. Go over the hill, down the road or across the county, but do your scouting. Find the places that attract deer like they did in Grandpa's day and start a new tradition there.

Scouting should not be a chore. You can "scout for deer" while pursuing other interests such as fishing, camping, turkey or small game hunting. Scouting is excuse enough for spending an early fall day in the woods, and what you learn about the woods from even one trip can turn your hunting season around. The track you're looking for, the rub, the scrape or trail that says "hunt here" is out there waiting for you — take some time and go look for it!

7. DEER STANDS

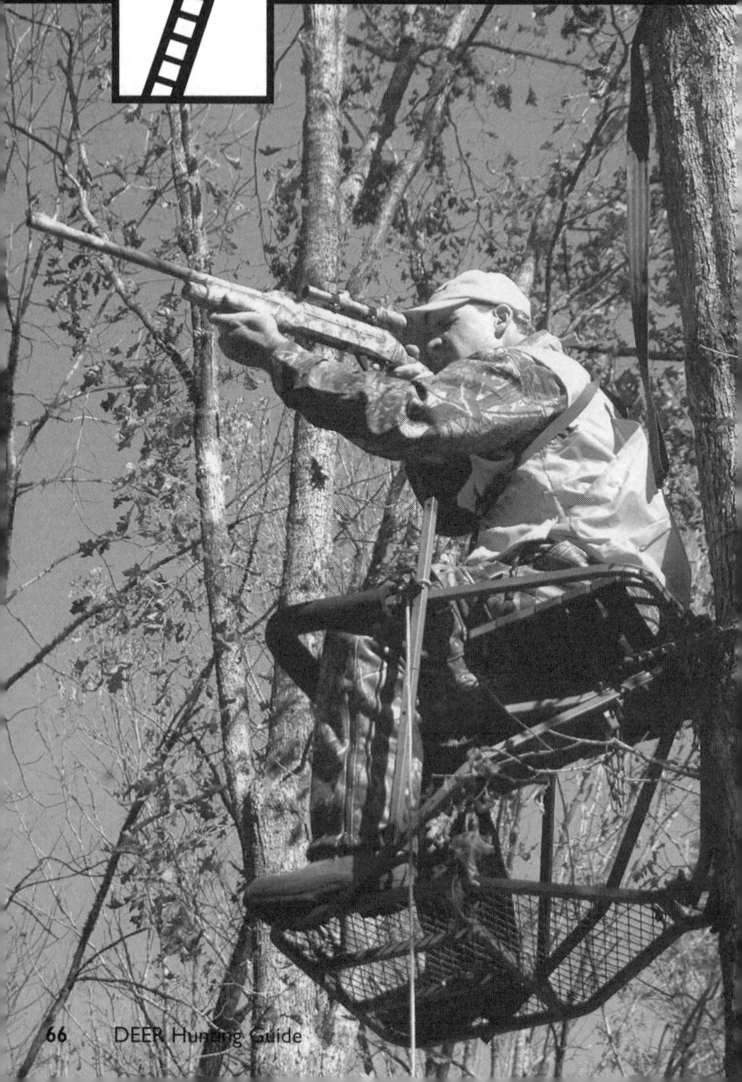

Perhaps no aspect of deer hunting has changed, improved and complicated the life of the hunter more than tree stands. Just 30 years ago, "tree stand" meant a few boards carelessly nailed to the crotch of a tree with an equally careless array of 2x4 rungs tacked to the trunk almost close enough to provide access to the uncomfortable platform or seat above. Most such stands were built in haste when a deer was spotted, hunted a few years with varying results and then left to decay. The skeletons of many of those early stands are still in the woods, some of them in places that are still excellent deer crossings.

Stand design is competitive and manufacturers keep creating bigger, better, more comfortable stands that are lightweight, strong, quiet and easy to transport.

Ladder Stands

The most popular type of deer stand at present is the ladder stand. These are normally metal, 12- to 16-feet high and lightweight, though they are intended for installation in a permanent location. Ladders may be one-piece, three-piece or in various configurations of rungs or steps. They are usually stable, solid and comfortable to hunt from, but they do have their drawbacks.

Ladder stands are normally installed so that the hunter faces the most likely approach lane of deer, a field edge or similar "high use" area. The drawback is that deer meander at will and, sooner or later, they're going to come from behind you. This puts the ladder stand hunter at a disadvantage because it's difficult (and unsafe) to stand up, turn around or shoot from the off side.

This has been such a problem for some that the natural progression was to tripod stands — three-legged, elevated stands that swivel on a pedestal. Popular in the West, where much of the deer hunting is done over vast stands of brushy cover with few trees, tripods are catching on the East as well in situations where they can be used without being spotted by or spooking incoming deer.

Hanging Stands

A hanging stand is simply a seat-and-strap assembly, often with an attached footrest, that is attached to the tree and accessed using pegs, steps, wraparound ladder or similar climbing device. Hanging stands are popular among hunters because of their small size, affordability and lightweight. A hunter can easily pack and carry two or three hanging stands and access devices into the woods and install them on his own in a single afternoon.

The drawbacks of hanging stands is that the seat is generally small, the anchoring system is often suspect (sometimes no more than friction straps and hooks) and the foot rest is often too small for maneuvering should a deer appear behind or to the hunter's off-side (over the right shoulder for right-handed shooters, for example.)

Climbing Stands

Many hunters now use climbing stands because they are lightweight, strong and comfortable. The hunter can carry the stand into the woods and simply climb into the tree of his choice.

Climbing stands are generally two-piece units (a seat and a foot rest) that are attached via cords or straps while in use. This keeps the footrest from slipping and leaving the seated hunter stranded in the tree. To ascend, the hunter climbs into the seat section facing the tree, attaches special foot-holds to his boots to keep the foot-rest section under control, and "climbs" the tree six inches to a foot at a time in the manner of a sloth or black bear.

An accomplished climber can arrive at his tree and be 20 feet up, ready to hunt, in 15 minutes.

Climbing stands have advanced to the point that the seat portion is broad and comfortable, the foot rest is solid and stable enough for the hunter to stand up and shoot behind or to the left or right rear, and quiet enough that the hunter can move about without alerting incoming deer.

The disadvantage of

climbing stands is that they are generally large, somewhat cumbersome and not good to carry through brush and briars. It's often best to transport climbing stands into the woods before the hunt, leave the stand at the base of the tree overnight and then return in the morning.

Safety Precautions

No elevated stand is 100-percent safe at all times. Tree-stand accidents are now the leading cause of death and injury among deer hunters.

Never climb a tree without a secure harness. It takes less than a minute to attach a harness and the procedure involved adds only a minute or two to the total climb time. Most hunters need only slip or fall once to realize the importance and value of a secure climbing harness, but, unfortunately, not all hunters use them.

Do not hunt from a tree stand of any type without a harness attached. A long day in a tree during deer season could include rain, snow, wind, fatigue and drowsiness. Any one of these could cause a slip, and a hunter who has been in a tree stand all day may not be in full control of his balance or faculties. One slip could mean disaster, but a secure harness will negate any damage other than the embarrassment of having used it!

Make certain the stand is secure, tight and operable before raising your gun or bow. Of course, guns and crossbows (where legal) should be unloaded and un-cocked while being lifted into the stand (usually by using a rope or strap). Because this procedure is often done before daylight, it is patently unsafe to elevate a loaded firearm or crossbow 20 feet or more into a tree. The rope could slip, the implement could bump against the tree or stand — the risk is too high for an accidental discharge.

Do not load or cock rifles, shotguns or crossbows until they are securely in your hands and pointed in a safe direction!

When leaving a tree stand for the day, carefully lower your gun, bow and other gear by rope, and then flex your arm and leg muscles to get the kinks out. Think about your exit strategy and carefully leave the stand using calculated hand and foot movements. Know where your rails, rungs and steps are before you commit to that next step! Most tree-stand accidents occur when the hunter is entering or leaving the stand, so think about what you are doing, take your time and move carefully. It only takes a few minutes to enter or leave a tree stand, but a mistake can cost you years of misery — even your life!

8. GROUND HUNTING

So many hunters now use tree stands, ladder stands or elevated box blinds that ground hunting is becoming a lost art. Still, it's safe to say that more deer have been taken by hunters on the ground than have been shot by hunters using elevated stands. Hunters who are patient, able to sit still under the scrutiny of approaching game and who know when to move (or not move) into position for a shot should be able to take deer from ground stands or blinds with no trouble.

For example, last season, I shot a nice 8-point buck in Georgia while gun hunting on the ground (range about 15 yards!), and another buck in Ohio with a crossbow (range about 5 yards!). In fact, all but a handful of the deer, bears, turkeys and other game I've shot over the last 40 years have been taken from the ground.

Free-Standing

I prefer to stand up while ground hunting, but sitting on a log, stump, rock or the bare dirt works well, too. In my later years I have become fond of a small foam seat cushion that fits in my daypack and keeps the errant root, rock or twig from annoying me, but in most cases I simply pick a large tree or blow down, back up against it and wait.

This is the basic tactic used by all still-hunters (meaning hunters who walk slowly through the woods in search of deer). Every so often you'll come to spot that just demands an investment of time — a plethora of tracks, trails, rubs or scrapes — and the hunter simply finds a suitable vantage point, sidles up to a convenient tree or bush and waits.

Whether the site is to be used for an hour or a week, preparation time is minimal.

- Scrape away leaves, snow and other debris from around your feet.
- Trim away any twigs, limbs or vines that impede your vision or movement.

It's not necessary to create a 10-foot clear-cut around the position, just clear away enough cover for a clean shot.

A passing deer will notice any hunter's presence sooner or later, but if you move quietly and slowly, and your gear is obscured, you will get the extra few seconds you'll need to make a well-aimed shot.

I have shot dozens of deer from positions such as this one. Some were 100 yards away; others were less than five yards away. Last year's Ohio buck (using a crossbow, a short-range implement) bounded up to me while escaping other hunters and stopped for a moment directly in front of me, broadside and totally unaware of my presence. In fact, the crossbow arrow passed through him and he actually watched it skitter away into the woods before he staggered off, mortally wounded, collapsing about 20 yards farther on.

The key to success in ground hunting is to stand still, be patient and pay attention. Investigate every sound and every movement. It may be a mouse, a chickadee or a squirrel that you hear, or it could be a deer. Verify! If it's non-game, relax and enjoy the show. If it's a deer, you have the drop on him and should be able to take an easy shot at your ease.

When a deer is approaching, wait for the animal's head to disappear behind a tree or bush. Raise your gun quickly, and then wait for the animal to move behind another obstacle before tilting your head to aim. That "raise and aim" sequence in the first few seconds of any hunter-deer encounter has saved the lives of many animals. Be patient — move slowly and pick your opportunities. A walking deer will be in range of any firearm for 100 yards in either direction, more in open woods. If you've practiced with your rifle or shotgun, you should be able to hit that heart-lung area out to at least 100 yards. Relax, wait for a good shot, and take it as soon as the opportunity is presented.

I am one who prefers to let deer come as close as possible before shooting. I always wait till the shot looks too easy, and then I let the deer advance another two steps before firing. It is more important to me that I make a good, clean, killing shot than risk anything less, and in 40 years I have not had to shoot a deer twice. And, the vast majority of those deer were taken from ground stands!

BLINDS

Ground Blinds

A "ground blind" can be as simple as a single bush in the ideal location, or as complicated as a roomy log-and-branch corral with seats, backrests and windbreaks. It's not necessary to build a blind complete with moat and drawbridge, although some hunters are willing to go that far!

A serviceable ground blind is simply a place to hide from approaching deer, and in fact if you build such a blind today and hunt from it tomorrow you will likely have problems because deer notice radical changes to their environment, and the sudden appearance of a ground blind (a large, hulking form that wasn't there yesterday) will frighten or at least alert every deer that comes by.

Permanent ground blinds should be constructed well before the season so deer have a chance to get used to their presence. Ideally, build your blind several weeks in advance using material you find on the ground nearby – logs, rocks, downed limbs and the like. Cutting of trees or trimming live trees is forbidden on most public lands, and the permission of the landowner should be sought before cutting any live wood on privately-owned properties. Cutting fresh trees (boughs or leafy branches) is not recommended for blind building because such cutting noticeably changes the habitat and creates shockingly obvious stumps and cut-off stubs that deer will see. Also, if you cut enough foliage you change the makeup of the forest in that area and may actually cause deer to avoid it.

Build your blind from the inside, not the outside. Many a fantastic blind has been built that, to the hunter's amazement and consternation, didn't have enough room inside for him, his gear and gun. The purpose of a blind is to allow a hunter to cover a 360-degree area, so check as you build to ensure that you can see all around you and that you will be able to shoot accurately at any deer that shows up from any direction.

Blinds should be thickly woven so small movements can't be seen and also high enough so that approaching deer won't see more than the top of your hat. The best blinds are unobtrusive, made of natural materials and allow the hunter some freedom of movement without spooking incoming deer.

Blinds of Opportunity

Somewhere between standing openly beside a tree or bush and tucking tightly inside a well-constructed ground blind are "blinds of opportunity." These can be large rocks, fallen trees, leaning logs or brush piles that happen to be in the precise place you need them to be. These can be hard to find in brushy areas, but old clear-cuts, wood-lots and forest tracts generally contain dozens of prime candidates.

When you find such an obstacle that is of use to you, simply clear away the detritus (leaves and branches on the ground), cut the few sprouts or limbs that affect your vision, tuck in and sit still. The advantage of such blinds is that they are already in place, deer are used to them and there's no work involved. They also offer protection from the wind and, in most cases, a solid rest for shooting.

My favorite such blind is in a patch of woods

where I frequently hunt other game. Over the years I have shot several deer, turkeys and squirrels and one coyote from this spot, which is nothing more than the uprooted trunk of a windblown oak. I did nothing in advance but find this spot to my liking. I have a little place cleared out for a comfortable seat, and I can see or hear approaching game from either side. The stand is good for another 10 years, even longer if the termites leave the tree alone. It doesn't get any easier than that!

Artificial Blinds

Many hunters are now turning to portable blinds for their deer hunting. These are essentially self-supporting tents designed to hold one or two hunters on stools or chairs. They have plenty of windows and openings for observing and shooting game, with the added advantage of a waterproof roof and sides for protection against the wind and rain.

All of the commercially-offered blinds I've seen are lightweight, easy to set up and comfortable. Some even have a built-in chair with an attached blind section that folds over and around it. Most manufacturers offer the blinds in various camouflage colors and white (for hunting on snow).

The advantages of these blinds is that all you have to do is find a spot to your liking, erect the blind and get in. There's no cutting, trimming or building to do, and approaching deer cannot see you or what you're doing even if they are standing right outside the blind. Photographers rave about these blinds and most won't enter the woods for wildlife viewing without one.

Also, these blinds are ideal for bad-weather hunting. Your gun and gear will be protected from the elements and you can even bring along a small heater, blanket or down bag for added warmth, a sensible consideration when hunting the late seasons in the cold, snowy regions of North America.

Still-Hunting

Still-hunting simply means walking slowly through deer habitat hoping to spot a deer before it sees you! There are situations where this technique is useless (such as in open woods during calm, still days when the leaves or snow are crunchy and loud), but there are times when it's a deadly tactic. Many hunters in the thick evergreen forests of the North Country still-hunt with great success because the cover is thick, the ground underfoot is quiet and deer are used to avoiding danger by sitting still and letting intruders or predators pass by.

Successful still-hunting begins with the right frame of mind. Because you are moving through the woods you are at a disadvantage. All animals, including deer, take sight and sound clues very seriously. Deer spend most of their time bedded or standing still, just looking and listening. Snap a twig and it will be heard – move too quickly and you will be noticed. And, because humans are generally very noisy, clumsy and impatient compared to the average chickadee, mouse or grouse, it's no wonder the most common sight a hunter sees is the bobbing white "flags" of departing deer.

If you're going to succeed at still-hunting, your hunt must begin the instant you leave the car or camp. When you are ready to enter the woods with your pack on your back and your rifle or shotgun in hand, stop for a moment and gather your wits, your senses and your focus. Clear your head of work issues, personal problems, worries and aggravations – save them for another time. Pause at the edge of the woods and rid your mind of anything but the game at hand. There are deer out there and your job today is to find them. Think about nothing else, pay attention to the signs you see and obey your own dormant predatory instincts. When you can hear the leaves rustling, when you are aware of dew dripping to the forest floor, and when your own footfalls sound like the pounding of elephants on the run, you're ready to enter the woods for a serious day of still-hunting.

Most hunters who claim to be still-hunting are fooling themselves. Their common faults are too much noise and too much movement. I can't tell you how many times I have been on a stand, on the ground in plain sight wearing an orange hat and coat, and have had a "still-hunter" walk right past me without noticing me! If you can't see a 200-pound pumpkin standing in full view on the ground, how do you expect to see a deer first? Odds are, you won't.

To be a successful still-hunter, you must be able to walk all day at a snail's pace, not so much covering a lot of ground but truly hunting the ground you do cover. When conditions are right (a little wind, some rain, dead silence muffled by wet leaves or snow) you can sneak through the woods and get surprisingly close to deer, possibly covering a mile or more in a morning. But, when it's quiet, dry and noisy afoot, you may not be able to cover more than a few hundred yards all day. To do so requires all the balance, stamina and focus of a world-class gymnast.

The job description of the still-hunter is clear: Walk very slowly and silently in short spurts of 10 to 20 yards. Stop, look and listen at each stop for at least 15 minutes. Stay longer if a spot "feels" right; if it is loaded with sign and you think a deer should be close by. Oftentimes they are, but they are playing the same game from their own perspective. Of course, only one can win!

Don't rush. Remember, you do not have to be anywhere at any particular time (nor do the deer). Go left, go right, meander in circles, or stay put. The deer are doing the same and sooner or later you are going to bump into each other. The important thing is to move slowly and silently, and be relentlessly looking for game at every step.

Some hunters move steadily through the woods in a straight line from Point A to Point B. While you may cover more ground this way and you will reach your destination sooner, you are actually telling the deer everything they need to know. Think about it: You're walking at a steady pace, you're headed in a distinct direction and you are not stopping to look around. Deer know enough to see that if they stand still you will walk right past them and not see them. I have witnessed this many times when I knew where deer were bedded or feeding as another hunter walked by. The deer would be alert and watchful, of course, but as long as the hunter continued on his course they were content to stay put and let him go on by.

Some hunters give up on stealth if the woods are noisy, but that's the sin of impatience. Believe it or not, it is possible to move through dry woods all day long without making a sound. It's a matter of being slow and deliberate in your steps. At times you may take only three or four steps and then have to stop for several minutes because the intensity level is so high. It is stressful to know that deer are nearby and one crack of a twig will send them bounding away. When I stop, I use the time to listen for deer moving around me and to scan every inch of the terrain ahead. I know they are out there and I want to see them first!

It is possible to walk up on deer even when the leaves are frozen and crackling like cornflakes. The key is to fool them through silence, stealth and alertness. A deer is not threatened unless it sees, hears or smells something nearby. If you are moving as slowly as possible, quiet as a shadow as you move through the woods, in most cases you will see or hear the deer first. Once they have seen or heard you, however, the game is over — and they win!

Impatience is the still-hunters greatest obstacle. Stay focused! The hunt is not over until the guns are unloaded for the day. Deer can be anywhere and may show up at any time, so hunt as if there is a nice buck behind every bush. Maintain a slow, steady, alert pace no matter how empty the woods appear and fight the urge to take off at a brisk walk just to get where you're going sooner.

For still-hunting:

- Dress lightly in clothing that is made of quiet fabrics. Cotton and wool are best; the modern fleeces are also good. You will be walking all day in a highly energized frame of mind, which generates more heat.
- Dress in layers and remove outer shells as you warm up.
- Wear a facemask and gloves because the human face and hands show up stark white and shine brightly against the muted colors of the forest.
- Wear lightweight rubber boots or well-worn leather or Gore-Tex boots. Footwear should be lightweight, flexible and have that certain "feel" that allows you to detect twigs, leaves, branches and other obstacles before they make that telltale "crunch" underfoot.

Though stainless steel barrels and actions are the rage these days, they are a risky choice for the still-hunter. You will move your rifle constantly as you maneuver through the woods, and on bright days the flash of metal parts can be seen for 100 yards or more. Even bright-finished blued barrels shine like beacons in the forest. Forget vanity and opt for matte black or camouflage finishes on metal parts if you intend to still-hunt. Every year I see hunters going by with their glittering stainless rifles in hand — they never see me, and I'm sure they bypass a lot of deer as well.

When still-hunting, the wind is a factor only

when the prevailing breeze is steady and strong. I have hunted throughout North America and have noticed that, no matter where I am from Idaho to Georgia to Maine, the wind can blow left, right and in circles, at varying speeds and directions with no real pattern a hunter can use. One time I released a bit of thistledown to track the wind. The down nearly touched the ground, swirled high over my head, curled back to about waist high, headed off into the woods in front of me and then came back on an updraft practically into my hand again. There is no way to monitor or thwart the wind in most woodland situations, so the best advice is to head into the prevailing winds (which run southwest to northeast in most of the eastern U. S., for example) and ignore the occasional gust that goes against the grain. Woods, mountains and river valleys create more wind problems, as does night or evening air currents.

You can't predict where the wind is going or in which direction it will be blowing 100 yards ahead, so don't waste time thinking about it.

Hunt thick cover – move slowly, look and listen. That's what deer do when the wind fails them, and that's all you have to do, too.

Stalking

Stalking is a unique deer-hunting tool that few hunters ever get to practice. Stalking involves a deer that you have seen and know the location of, but must sneak closer to in order to have a shot. In

most cases this is an open-country process because thick-cover deer are difficult to spot at long range and even more difficult to stalk because of wind, noisy conditions, land barriers and other obstacles.

The process is a simple one on paper. See the deer, utilize available cover to get close and take the shot when you run out of cover. Easy, right? Sometimes it is, but not always. Elk, moose and mule deer are most inclined to stay put long enough for a hunter to execute a stalk, but whitetails tend to be nervous and unpredictable. They will get up and move for no apparent reason, perhaps because their internal "danger monitor" tells them they've been in the same place too long. Or, they simply move along in order to feed or bed elsewhere, leaving the intrepid stalker in frustration after investing time and energy on a stalk of a now-empty field or clear-cut.

If you know the area well and know in which direction deer are most likely to move when threatened, you can combine a stalk with an ambush setup. Simply work your way into the area you expect to see deer as they move along and wait for them to show up. When the trick works it's extremely productive.

Tracking

Tracking deer is a popular and productive technique in the north woods, primarily in areas where hunter access is unrestricted and frequent snowfalls are the norm during deer season.

The short version of "tracking" is simple enough: Find the track of a deer you want to hunt and follow it to the end! Most hunters find the initial discovery of a huge, splayed buck track to be very exciting, but maintaining that same level of excitement while following the trail over hill and dale, through swamps, clear-cuts and bogs, over mountains and through brushy valleys can be a major challenge.

This is a refined version of still-hunting. The difference is that you can move faster when the deer is walking or loping, and you know the deer is there — you just have to catch up to him before nightfall. Some tracking jobs end in an hour or two, while others may go on for days. The renowned Larry Benoit wrote that he spent 13 days on the track of a big buck.

If you are determined to take the buck you are tracking and will accept no other, you may end up spending the entire season (or what's left of it) on his trail. The typical one-week vacation hunt may not be enough time to get the job done, but in some instances you can be back home by noon on the first day. The game plays itself out at its own pace and you're either in or you're out. Decide if you want to play before you start and then maintain the determination to get the job done.

You must be in tip-top shape to be a successful tracker. You are challenging not only the buck ahead of you, but the terrain around you, which in many cases can be thick, wet and endless.

Proper clothing for tracking means light, wicking materials. You are going to be walking all day and sweating profusely. Heavy clothing is not necessary at any point in the hunt, and if you kill your buck you're going to have to drag him out, which means more work, more sweat. Don't overdress for tracking – you'll either quit in an over-heated swoon or start tossing expensive clothing to the wind. Wear lightweight rubber boots (with snow on the ground you're going to get wet!) and bring two or three pairs of fresh socks. Change socks every few hours for comfort and for the mental boost you need to keep going.

Carry a lightweight day pack containing:

- ❏ Compass and map
- ❏ Water purifier or pump
- ❏ Granola or chocolate bars for quick energy
- ❏ Knife (a Leatherman SuperTool is ideal)
- ❏ Rope (10 feet).
- ❏ Socks (Three or four pairs)
- ❏ Space blanket or small tarp
- ❏ Waterproof matches
- ❏ Cup.
- ❏ Band-Aids for blisters.

Travel light and fast — know where you're going and drink plenty of water throughout the day. Tracking deer in snow is all work all day and you must be up to the task.

Generally, when a deer shows signs of meandering he's looking for a place to bed. Be alert, be ready — this is the most likely time that you'll see him. Expect him to circle back above or below you and watch for him to be watching for you!

Tracking is great fun when it goes as planned, but expect to lose the game a lot more often than you win! Learn from your mistakes and eventually you will master this challenging and satisfying technique.

One of the most mysterious and misunderstood aspects of deer hunting is the issue of scent control: What do deer smell, how do they react to it and what can hunters do about it?

Suffice it to say that, from a deer's point of view, hunters stink! It doesn't much matter what we wear, what we do or how often we shower, nothing a human brings into the woods smells "natural" to deer. We try, we come up with new stuff every year and we do a good job of fooling ourselves, but the fact is that, so far, there has yet to be a product or procedure that a deer can't sniff out!

The basic rule of thumb in deer hunting is to hunt or face upwind because deer move into the prevailing wind while traveling from place to place. As a "rule of thumb," this is great. The problem is that there are days with no wind, lots of wind, gusting wind, winds blowing in all four directions at random ... and we have to be out there under all these conditions because deer season falls where it does and we can't pick and choose ideal conditions for every trip. You take what you get on the day you go and you make the most of it.

The good news is that deer are killed on every day of the season, rain or shine, hot or cold, wind or no wind. Deer must eat, bed and, during the rut, breed regardless of climatic conditions. Deer are shot in blinding rainstorms, blizzards, gusty post-storm winds and on calm, still days when a downy feather can fall straight to the ground from 20 feet in the air.

Hunters can't control the weather or the luck of the draw in choosing the one day when every condition seems to be wrong. We can, however, control what we do, wear and bring into the woods to minimize the effect of scent on approaching deer.

Clothing Selection

Before you even leave the house for the day, consider putting a complete set of clean, unscented hunting clothes in a plastic bag and leave it in your vehicle till you get to your hunting site. You and I may be used to normal household odors (cooking smells, chemical cleaners, deodorants, soaps, shampoos and the like) but deer are not. If such scents do not outright frighten the animals, they alert them

to your presence, which is just as bad, because a deer that's detected your presence is not going to be fooled by anything else you can do. All the deer will do now is look and listen till he finds the source of the unusual scent, and then bound away — or simply slink into thick cover without you ever knowing he was around.

The odors associated with smoking, drinking and fast foods are very strong and pervasive. I do not smoke or drink, yet I can smell the lingering odors of alcohol and tobacco on other hunters from 20 or more feet away. I am sure deer can pick up those odors from much greater distances. You're not going to fool them by not smoking on your way into your stand — the scent of last night's cigar is going to precede you in the wind.

The only solution to odor problems is to enter the woods with a clean body (use unscented soaps and shampoos) and change into unscented clothing when you reach the woods. I have my doubts that anything manmade smells "natural" to deer, animals that live their entire lives in nature surrounded by "natural" odors, but anything the hunter can do to minimize intrusive odors is a plus.

Elevate Your Stand

Perhaps the easiest thing a hunter can do is climb into an elevated stand, get well above the prevailing wind and hope that his scent, that of his stand, rifle and other gear, will be carried above and beyond approaching deer. This may be a great tactic in flat, low country where winds are constant and predictable, but in mountainous areas, rolling hills and deep valleys it is all but impossible to predict the direction of the wind on any given day.

To test the vagaries of wind direction, I have released milkweed silk from 20 feet up in a tree and watched it spin, float and drift high, low, back and forth until, eventually, it came to rest on the ground. I have conducted such tests from various elevations and in all kinds of hunting conditions and the end result seems to be that there's no guarantee that a deer won't smell you before you can take a shot at it. Rifle hunters have an advantage in that they can make killing shots on alerted deer at a longer range, but short-range hunters (muzzleloaders, and shotgun hunters) can expect to encounter problems with scent throughout the season.

We can hope for the best on any given day, but on those days when you don't see or hear a thing in the woods, don't be shocked to find that your scent was being carried to the deer on the wind and the animals simply avoided your area.

Vary Your Approach To Your Stand

Knowing that scent can be carried a long way through the woods, a good tactic is to approach your stand from the downwind side even if it means taking a wide detour to avoid saturating the area upwind of your stand with scent.

When you are dressed in unscented clothing and are ready to go to your stand, stop a moment and consider the prevailing wind. If it's blowing from your stand to you, head directly for your stand. If the wind is blowing from you to your stand, consider taking a more circuitous route in order to avoid broadcasting your presence to bedded deer via your scent. This may certainly mean taking a longer, perhaps more difficult route, but in most cases such a detour is worthwhile. Of course, be sure your detour does not spread your scent across possible bedding areas.

- Look for the approach that has the least amount of prime cover, such as open woods, highways and open stream bottoms.
- Plan your approach so that you disturb or alert as few deer as possible.

Remember, if bedded deer catch your scent from a distance they are likely to get up and move elsewhere. In most cases you won't even know they were there! Deer spend their lives evading danger, and sometimes it's simply a matter of walking away at the first sign of trouble. Deer that smell you but don't see or hear you may be inclined to stop and wait for that second set of assurances (sight and smell, smell and sound or sight and sound), and those are the deer that you see bounding away with tails held high.

Cover Scents

There are many ways to manipulate scent distribution in the woods. You can use:

- Attractors (lures that bring deer into range).
- Common or "comfort" odors (urines, inter-digital musks and tarsal glands).
- Cover scents (food or other non-threatening odors that deer would not consider a threat).

Years ago, hunters simply dumped the contents of a scent bottle on a convenient stump or log, perhaps sprinkling some on their boot heels and called it good. Apple scents were popular (even in areas where there were no apples!), and acorn, corn and similar foods scents were standard shelf items during deer season. None of these concoctions surfaced as "guaranteed" deer attractants or cover scents. In fact, most of them had no impact at all on the deer herd!

Modern delivery systems include:
- Cotton-filled canisters
- Wicks of all sorts
- Heating units — smoke "lures" that burn like a patio insect repellent. In most cases, hunters place scented wicks or cotton-filled canisters at various locations about 20 yards away from their stands.

Other tricks include dragging a scent-soaked cotton ball or rag on the ground (attached to a boot heel or boot laces) to simulate a deer moving through the woods; making false scrapes, beds or rubs; and using life-sized deer decoys with appropriate scents applied. All of these have been known to work at times, but none of them have been shown to be constantly, continuously effective for deer in every situation. To be honest, the jury has long been out on the effectiveness of scents and lures.

I am not sure that using something to attract a meandering deer's attention as it approaches your stand is necessarily going to work for you because the deer is now alerted, searching for the source of the odor and ready to flee. For many years I surveyed the hunters who took the top 50 bucks in Maine with an eye on how they did it so other hunters could learn from their success. Over the 10 years that I conducted the survey, not one big buck was taken using scents or lures; or tree stands; or camouflage cloth-

ing, for that matter (Maine is a mandatory orange state). Many of those hunters never made it to their stands — the buck showed up before they got there! Others hurried to the woods before or after work and just bumped into their trophy along the way, and one hunter took three top-ranked bucks in a row from the same roadside field he passed on the way to work in the morning! In no case did a hunter see the buck prior to the season, or even know such a deer was in his hunting area. They were simply in the right place at the right time and ready to shoot when the opportunity presented itself — probably the common bottom line in most go-it-alone, non-commercial hunts in North America.

Scent manufacturers are very proud of their products, ingredients, collection methods and "freshness" claims, and most of them take their business very seriously. I think that each situation is different and unique, and that individual deer will react to scents and lures depending on how he feels at the moment he encounters them. However, one year I called every major scent manufacturer advertising at the time and asked them to guarantee their products — assure every hunter who used their product and followed the directions that they would kill a deer using it. Every one of them balked at the idea! Sure, they have the best ingredients, the finest captive deer herds, the best-looking ad campaigns — but would they guarantee you a deer if you bought their product? No!

That said, it may be that using cover scents for deer using deer-attracting odors can work for the simple reason that those odors are not foreign to deer and may cause them to drop their guard long enough for the hunter to make a killing shot.

Anything that lures a deer into range or stops him for a shot is worth investigating, however, deer are complex animals that have been dodging predators for eons. They are not easy to fool under any circumstances, and scents alone are not going to do it!

Suffice it to say that deer scents and lures may work on occasion to attract or calm approaching deer. There is no miracle in a bottle yet for deer hunters, but anything can happen at any given time, and so these products are certainly worth investigating when conditions warrant it. If nothing else, they will get you into the woods where the action is, and that alone is half the battle!

SURVIVAL
KIT

The deer-hunting industry has grown by leaps and bounds since the infamous 5,000-year-old man (a hunter found frozen in a glacier in the Alps) set out with a handmade bow, a knife and some seeds to eat. The fact that he was dressed in animal skins and had a skin quiver and shoes makes it obvious that gear and gadgets are not necessarily the key to deer-hunting success.

Between minimalists (the knife and string crowd) and gadget geeks (who bring two of everything into the woods including the kitchen sink), there is some middle ground. After all, hunting is a sport, a hobby and a pleasurable pursuit for most hunters. Despite the universal appeal of venison, buckskin and a nice set of antlers on the wall, most hunters enjoy their time in the woods and, successful or not, head for home feeling at least as good as when they left. In most states, some 90 percent of hunters fail to fill their tags, some for many years on end, yet they return the next fall with renewed enthusiasm and optimism.

It is possible to spend an entire day in the woods with only a knife and a gun, and I have done it many times. In leaner times, my father and I spent a week in the wilds of Maine existing on oatmeal, peanut butter sandwiches and cans of pea soup.

You can rough it and still come home with a buck tied to the roof rack, and everyone should do it the hard way … once! But, to enjoy deer hunting, a few items, lightweight and easily fit into a day pack, should be carried into the woods..

Proper clothing for the job is mandatory.
More hunters quit the woods (thereby saving the hides of countless deer!) because their hands or feet were cold. There was a time when the only choices for hunters were cotton long johns, wool pants, flannel shirts and heavy wool coats. These days, the lists of outdoor clothing is endless, with new products and designs appearing each season.

Lighter is better, of course, especially if you plan to spend the day walking or hiking. In fact, it is better to dress in less and be a little cool while standing than to bulk up with heavy, thick clothing and break into a major sweat after 50 yards. When you reach your stand, you'll be drenched in sweat, and that sweat will turn to ice water in minutes.

Each hunter must take measure of his own comfort level and, with practice and experience, find that combination of underwear, outer clothing, boots, gloves, jackets and hats that will get the job done.

When choosing hunting clothing:
- Prepare for rain and wind — A water-resistant shell combats both.
- Cold hands — Trigger-finger gloves with added chemical hand warmers are good in below-zero cold.
- Cold feet — Heavy, insulated boots will wear you out over the course of a day, but in lightweight, non-insulated boots, your feet may turn to ice in an hour. Know your personal comfort level and purchase socks, boots and liners to match.

In dressing for the day's hunt:
- Think about the weather conditions (plan for the worst!).
- Recognize your own comfort level, know your personal limitations (cold feet, cold hands, etc.).
- Never leave camp without the necessities. Otherwise, you could face a miserable day in the woods; or, demoralized by the cold, wind or rain, abort the hunt. Be sensible, be honest about yourself, dress properly and plan to be in the woods all day.

Sensible Supplies

I have hunted deer throughout North America in every sort of weather, climatic condition and topography. There was a time (when I was much younger) when I would go into the woods before dawn, hunt all day and not return to camp till after dark – and brought nothing into the woods with me but my rifle, a knife and a length of rope. I hunted hard, I shot plenty of deer ... and I was miserable all day. Not only was I hungry, tired and cold but I often suffered (unknowingly) from the effects of hypothermia and dehydration. I didn't drink any water, and I often didn't move a muscle all day as I waited on my stand, many times from before dawn till after dark. I shot deer, certainly, because I was there and ready for action, but that kind of hunting is not pleasant.

The other extreme, of course, is weighting yourself down with so much extra "comfort" gear

(a Thermos, heavy sandwiches, canned items and snacks) that you can hardly walk in the woods. And, you spend more time (and make more noise) nibbling on goodies than you do hunting. I know hunters who, after settling down to a fine picnic at noon had the buck of a lifetime walk by as their rifle leaned up against a nearby tree!

Nowadays I hunt as hard but I enjoy it more. I bring a day pack that always contains a few energy bars or apples, a quart of water, a small gas stove and some tea or coffee in individual bags. Somewhere around 11 a.m. when the woods seem to be "empty" and wildlife activity seems to have subsided, I break out my stove, brew up a hot beverage and nibble on a snack. Sometime around 2 p.m., just before I expect deer to get up and start moving around again, I'll have another cup of tea or coffee (or two) and another snack. That's all I need to keep me alert and on track. It feels great to stop and take a break on those cold autumn days when you can still see your breath hanging in the air at high noon!

You may want to eat more, drink more or have more variety, and that's fine. ***Carry in all you want but remember that the goal of each trip is to bag a deer, not have a buffet dinner!*** Minimize your selections, bring items that are quick and easy (and quiet!) to prepare and eat, and remember to maintain your vigilance at all times. If you are in deer country, expect to see deer at any time. They do not take breaks and they have no sympathy for careless hunters!

For example, a few years ago in Ohio I was hunting the Shawnee State Forest special blackpowder deer hunt and had stopped at the edge of a clearcut for my noon break. With my rifle in my lap I brewed some tea, ate an apple and a granola bar and considered my next move. Just then a fat doe walked up, not five yards away, oblivious of my presence. Her face was covered with foam and her eyes and ears were focused on the woods behind her. I knew what that meant!

I set my teacup down, picked up my rifle and waited. Right behind the doe came a tremendous 10-point buck, head down and grunting like a barnyard pig. I silently thumbed the hammer back, took careful aim and fired. As the smoke cleared I calmly finished my snack, got up and recovered my trophy, which was lying dead just a few yards away! *The moral: Always pay attention, even at snack time!*

Leave It As You Found It

Everything you bring into the woods should be brought back out. Do not leave cans, bottles, wrappers, bags or boxes in the woods. Burn paper items where you sit (where legal) or stash your trash in your pack for disposal at home or camp. *You found the woods in pristine condition when you arrived — be sure you leave it the same way!*

Don't Get Lost!

There is no reason for any hunter to carry enough gear to survive a month in the wilderness in anticipation of getting lost, because, of the millions of hunters who do enter the woods each year, a scant handful ever get truly "lost." Of those few, only one or two will endure more than a night or two in the woods before being rescued. There are few incidents in which hunters become so lost or injured that they must fend for themselves for weeks on end. In fact, in 2005 some 14 Pennsylvania boaters lost their lives in watercraft accidents, but not one hunter in all of North America died in the woods purely as a result of being "lost."

Should a hunter find himself far from camp at the end of a particularly trying day, the gear in his pack should sustain him till he finds his way out of the woods or is rescued. It doesn't take much to survive overnight in the woods if you maintain your composure and have faith in the highly-trained teams of rescue personnel who will soon be coming out to find you.

But, If You Do Get Lost . . .

Odds are you are never going to get "lost" in the woods while deer hunting. For one thing, few areas in North America are truly "wild" anymore. You can see the lights of distant towns, phone towers or highways from just about anywhere, and there are few places in the Lower 48 states, at least (where most of the deer hunting takes place) where you will not find a road or trail of some sort.

Of course, it would be foolhardy to go to a remote hunting cabin or campsite and simply strike off into the woods without referring to a compass or studying a map of the area. Know where the lakes, streams, mountains and logging roads are. Stow a laminated copy of the map in your pack and refer to it as you hunt. You're not going to travel very far in most cases before encountering game, so there's no practical reason to head out beyond the last road, trail or waterway in search of game. But, if you do wander off and get "turned around," the procedure is the same whether you're a mile off the road or 20 miles off the beaten path.

Stop Walking,
Assess Your Situation!

The best insurance against getting truly lost in the first place is to tell someone where you are going, when you intend to return, where you are going to park your vehicle and what area you intend to hunt. This is all a rescue team needs to know. And, if you hunt where you said you'd be, sit tight and build a fire, rescuers will find you in no time at all. The problem becomes complicated when hunters panic, try to outwit the system or think that, once lost, they can find their own way out of the woods. Wandering aimlessly through the woods (night or day) is not going to do you any good, especially when, as normally happens, you come upon some fresh human tracks, get excited about being found and then discover that the tracks you have discovered are your own!

At the point that you realize you're going in the wrong direction or don't honestly know where you are, keep your wits about you.

- Sit down and stay where you are. Don't wander in circles.
- Build a smokey fire and let the rescue wheels begin to turn.
- Build a weatherproof shelter of limbs, boughs or even chunks of snow or sod.

Searchers will find you!

Simple and Functional

Most new hunters make the mistake of trying

to carry enough gear to thwart every possible disaster that could befall a lost hunter, and imaginations run wild when the topic is discussed around the kitchen table. For example, most "survival kits" contain, among other cool stuff, items like fishing gear, snare wire, sewing needles, glue and a pencil. Having been a participant in the search-and-rescue of several lost hikers, hunters and campers, I have trouble thinking of even one who stopped to fish, snare a rabbit, sew a button back on his shirt, repair something with glue or write a letter. This is the stuff of kitchen table survivalists!

For lost hunters, "survive" means to stay alive till rescuers come – and fishing, snaring and sewing are not high on the list of things to do!

Sure, you could fill your pack with these and other important survival tools (and camping supply houses wish you would!). However, you can't carry enough gear for every eventuality and still concentrate on hunting. The truth is that you can survive comfortably for days with very little peripheral gear and easily find your way out of the woods tomorrow or the next day. Few lost deer hunters have had to cope with longer periods of isolation, injured or not. If you leave camp one day and don't return that night, people are going to know about it and will be concerned. Wives, friends, fellow hunters or neighbors will certainly notify the authorities and the search-and-rescue wheels will begin to turn!

In anticipation of someday having to spend a night in the woods, the following items should be in every hunter's pack on every trip:

- ❏ A sharp knife (a Leatherman SuperTool or similar multi-blade tool is ideal).
- ❏ 50 feet of nylon rope (for aid in construction of a simple lean-to shelter).
- ❏ An 8'x10' plastic tarp (for a sleeping bag or even more comfortable shelter).
- ❏ A laminated map of the area you're hunting.
- ❏ A compass (and knowledge of its use).
- ❏ A water bottle with purification tablets.
- ❏ A tin cup for heating water.
- ❏ Tea or coffee in single-use bags.
- ❏ 100 waterproof matches with a small container of tinder.
- ❏ A small whistle or metal mirror.
- ❏ Flashlight

With the above items, which can easily fit into a small day pack or fanny pack, a lost hunter can build an emergency shelter, start a fire and keep himself hydrated for several days. The average human can live 30 days without food (you'll be hungry, of course, but you won't "starve" even if you must spend one or two nights in the woods without food). Drink plenty of water (purify or boil any water you intend to drink) and take the time to make yourself a cup of tea or coffee simply because doing so forces you to stop worrying, stay busy and rationally consider your options.

The whistle or mirror may be used to signal search crews should you be injured or otherwise unable to continue on your own. Just sit tight, feed the fire (tossing the occasional green bough or wet wood into the flames — during daylight, of course — to create a smoke signal for searchers), drink your tea and relax. Let the rescue crews worry about where you are and how to find you — it's their job, they're trained for it and they love to find their subjects happy, healthy and alive!

Anything else you bring into the woods is unnecessary from a practical point of view. Fill your pack with snacks, gadgets and "survival" gear if you are willing to carry it all, but surviving in the wild is not difficult if you have a shelter, heat and water. Relax, savor the experience; think up exciting things to tell everyone when you get back. Consider an unexpected night in the woods a challenge to be met and an enjoyable experience, one that you're prepared for and ready to accept.

11. AFTER THE SHOT

No hunter appreciates the pre-trip preparation, gun and ammo selection, sighting-in process and target choice like the one who has just fired a shot at a trophy buck. There is nothing worse than the sinking feeling that you have either missed or, even worse, wounded and lost what may be the only deer you're going to see this year. Don't let this happen to you!

To avoid all the grief, aggravation and disappointment that comes with a botched shot, force yourself to take your pre-hunt practice seriously. When sighting in, accept nothing less than holes-touching accuracy, especially at 25, 50 and 100 yards. At longer range, work to get your bullets to fall into a 3-inch circle. At 250 yards, the standard deer rifle should be able to place all its shots into an 8-inch circle (about the size of a paper plate). Most experienced riflemen can do better, but certainly do not settle for less! If you do not know where your bullets are going you are likely to miss or wound a deer when one shows up, and what happens next is only going to make matters worse.

When you do get a shot at a deer, you can shorten the period of dismay, disappointment and anxiety by knowing in advance where you want to shoot the deer and making the shot count. You do not have to shoot at a deer the instant you see it, nor do you have to take iffy shots at obscured targets. Wait! Wait for an open, standing broadside shot and place your sights or crosshairs on the area just behind the deer's shoulder and halfway up the body. If your gunsight screws are tight and haven't been "adjusted" since you were at the range, your bullet will strike somewhere in the "vitals" of the deer (heart, lung, liver area) and he will be dead when you get to him.

Watch for Signs of A Hit

Few deer fall down dead at the shot, although it happens from time to time. Most often, however, especially with large-caliber rifles, muzzleloaders and shotgun slugs, the animal will hunch up, stagger, turn around, lower its tail or head, or otherwise show evidence of being struck. The animal will often remain on its feet, perhaps even bounding off with tail held high as if unhurt.

If you did not sight in properly or have no faith in your equipment, how are you going to feel at this instant? Inexperienced hunters will offer a cursory look around, find no blood and conclude that they had missed, leaving the dying deer to feed the coyotes. Even a well-hit animal can travel long distances — every situation is unique and nothing is cast in stone. Your job is to find that deer no matter what, and the job is made easier if you are confident that your bullet hit where you aimed it. To have that level of assurance, wait for the best shot and stay focused on your target. You can get excited about antlers, body weight and the thrill of tagging your deer later!

When you are shooting at a deer, keep your eye on the job at hand. Nothing you have done prior and nothing you will do later is as important as putting that bullet, ball or slug exactly where it needs to go. When you are sure you've made a good hit, the follow-up process is routine and satisfying.

Last season, for example, I shot five deer in three different states. None of them fell dead at the shot, yet I was not worried about finding any of them. The best one, an 8-point buck hit behind the shoulder with a 100-grain PowerPoint bullet from my Ruger No. 1 in .243 Winchester, made a tremendous leap and ran headlong into a brushy creek bottom, but I knew before I stood up that I would find him lying dead somewhere down below. I simply gathered my gear, found the place where the buck was standing at the shot, followed the copious blood trail and walked easily downhill to where the buck lay dead, about 50 yards away.

Another buck was shot just as he was about to leap an old barbed-wire fence. He made the jump, fell on his face, got up and disappeared, but I had held my crosshairs halfway up and right behind the shoulder — I knew I'd find him in short order, and actually spotted his white belly fur lying about 30 yards away as I crossed the fence where he'd jumped it.

The Tracking Process

All well-hit deer will die as a result of a hunting bullet through the heart-lung area, but some will go much farther than others. The process of finding gunshot deer, however, is the same in every case. Let's assume you've waited for a good shot, pulled the trigger and are confident that your bullet found its mark. Now what?

The first thing to do is go to the place where you hit the deer and stop. Look carefully for blood, hair or some other sign of a hit. **Do not move until you find evidence of a hit.** Sometimes there will be copious amounts of blood and hair, but many times there will be a few hairs and a light spray of blood on the far side of where the deer had been standing. This evidence can be difficult to find when the ground is bare and dry (or wet), but it is there. Find it! There could be clots of blood, bits of organs, skin or hair, but any gunshot will leave evidence. **DON'T MISS IT!**

When you find blood:
- Mark that spot with a piece of flagging, your hat or bend a nearby branch in an obvious manner.
- Find the next spatter of blood or hair, scuffed tracks or other sign.
- Stop and mark the spot, and then look for more blood.

In most cases, you will find your deer within 50 yards or so, but individual circumstances are infinite — it doesn't matter if the deer is a foot or a mile away, the process is the same. Find blood, mark the spot, find the next spot, mark it ... continue this process till you reach your deer. If you shot the animal with a rifled slug or bullet halfway up behind the shoulder, he will not be far away and he will be dead when you reach him.

Any other shot leaves room for uncertainty, which is why I recommend taking the "money" shot behind the shoulder. Hunters who take head, neck, spine or high shoulder shots often end up in marathon tracking sessions that sometimes end in disappointment. To me, the risk is too high for any other approach. But, when you decide to pull the trigger you commit yourself to finding the animal at all costs, and that can include staying out all night, picking up the trail again next morning and tracking all the next day. *A wounded deer can travel for hours and will cover a lot of ground!* You'll make your own tracking job easier if you maintain your composure and put your bullet where it belongs. There is no excuse for sloppy, inaccurate shooting. Don't even go into the woods if you are not ready for the responsibility. A deer is a living thing, a valuable trophy bolstering a far-reaching industry. Every buck or doe deserves to be treated with respect, and a clean kill is just the beginning.

Tricks of the Trade

Ideally, your wounded buck will leave a blood trail a blind man could follow, as the saying goes ... but not always. One deer I shot in Maine years ago was stretched out on his hind legs while trying to eat some Old Man's Beard, a common type of moss that dangles from dead tree limbs in wet areas. When I shot, the deer was fully extended from head to toe, but when he came down his skin slid over the bullet holes and he ran out of sight, leaving no blood, hair or any other sign ... on snow! Other than the fact that I was confident I'd hit him, there was nothing to prove it but myriad tracks in the snow.

However, I had done my job, I'd waited for a clean, open shot, and I had aimed carefully as I pulled the trigger. I was sure I had him, I just didn't know where he'd end up.

I spent a long and fitful night waiting for dawn, and it didn't help to know my hunting partners were sure I'd missed. "Forget about it – those things happen," they said. I did not agree, and suffered the long night with anguish. At daylight I was back at my spot and started to recall the details of the event. It turned out that I had been looking for the deer in the area where I'd first seen it, not where I'd taken the shot! It was a matter of only 20 feet, but it made all the difference. I refocused my search, began looking for blood nearer to where I'd taken the shot and found the buck about 20 yards farther east than I'd expected. He was stone dead, lying where he had fallen the night before. The cold and snow kept him fresh enough that I was able to recover all the meat, but the best part was that I had faith in my shot and had followed up on it.

Tracking deer in snow can be much easier than finding blood on bare ground, but not always. A lung-shot deer may spray a great deal of blood across the snow in very fine droplets, and it may take some searching to find the deer's direction of travel.

Blood on fall leaves can be difficult to find, even in daylight. To help in these situations, wrap a length of toilet paper around your hand, get down on all fours and start patting the leaves with the tissue. Any blood spatters will show up quickly on the soft, white paper.

At night, use a bright light or lantern to follow blood trails. Fresh blood shows up very well after dark. Today's LED penlights and headlamps make following nighttime trails easy – just be sure to have spare batteries on hand!

Some states allow the use of tracking dogs for finding lost deer, and their recovery rate is phenomenal. It's best to contact these groups before the season opens (try the state fish and wildlife department or local game warden for a list of volunteers) so you have the name and number of a participant on hand should you need him.

Group Tracking

It's often the common urge for a group of hunters to run off in various directions in an effort to be the first one to find a lost deer, but a more productive system starts with appointing a "track master." This is simply one individual who takes charge of the process, keeps track of the evidence and makes sure no one is inadvertently obliterating tracks, blood or other sign.

For best results, the group should start out single file and proceed to the site where the shot took place. Then, the hunt master asks one person to stand at the place where the first blood is found until the second source of sign is uncovered. Sign should be marked with flagging, broken boughs or blazes on trees, but only the hunt master should be allowed to mark trees, examine blood sign and make a decision on how to proceed. Otherwise, you'll have trackers going in every direction hoping to be the first one to find the lost deer, and in the process they may accidentally obliterate tracks, blood or other sign.

The bottom line in tracking (alone or with helpers) is: *Go slow, mark each track or blood spatter and do not proceed past the last bit of sign.* It can be a slow process, especially in the rain or at night, but the job has to be done and the best way to do it is logically and methodically. Remember, your buck is out there somewhere – it's just a matter of finding him based on the clues he's left behind.

The Hunter's Responsibility

It is every hunter's ethical responsibility to decide when to take a shot and then, having decided to shoot, to finish the job. Mistakes or carelessness on the hunter's part are not the fault of the deer! If you take a chance and try a marginal shot, expect things to go wrong but take the responsibility for your actions and find that deer! In most cases, mortally wounded deer are not going to survive the injury. Deer do make it through the winter with shot-off legs, jaws and tails, and some survive for years in such condition. Discovering what a deer can endure is not our goal, however. It's already been done too many times! If you choose to shoot at a deer and things go awry, take charge, invest all the time available and do what you must to recover that animal.

Deer shot in the heart-lung area will die quickly, though in most cases out of sight. Deer that are shot in the rear of the liver, stomach, intestines or rear quarter may travel for hours and cover a lot of ground leaving little sign to follow. It will be difficult to recover poorly-shot deer, but you must accept the responsibility and do all you can to resolve it. Call friends, experienced hunters, a game warden or a deer recovery specialist and make every effort to find that deer!

Losing a wounded deer is never a good experience and throws a pall over any hunting camp. ***Don't be the one who has to report a wounded, lost deer!***

12. FIELD DRESSING YOUR DEER

You've made a good shot and found your deer. Good job! For safety's sake, approach your downed deer from behind and above its shoulders. Move in slowly with your gun still loaded (but with the safety on). **_Watch the animal for signs of life._** If its eyes are open and there are no signs of breathing or other movement, the animal is likely dead. Touch the deer's rump with your foot and wait for a reaction. If nothing happens, this phase of the hunt is over.

If the deer appears to be breathing or moving, is blinking its eyes or attempts to rise, you must shoot the animal again immediately. Administer a shot at the base of the skull, just behind the ear. Head shots are unnecessarily damaging and unsightly, and body shots will simply ruin meat. Some taxidermists do not like the behind-the-ear shot because it can create a large hole in the hide, but recovery of the deer is most important. Hides can be repaired or substitute hides may be used for a mount – you can't mount a deer that gets up and runs away from you!

Fortunately, 99 percent of heart-lung shot deer will be dead when you catch up to them. The only deer I've had to shoot a second time were bucks I'd hit in the neck, head or lower chest — and thankfully few of those!

Congratulations! You've accomplished something only 10 percent of this year's hunters will achieve, and you have a right to be proud. Enjoy this moment, let the adrenalin flow, take some pictures and pause to admire and appreciate your trophy. The first thing I do after confirming a kill is affix my license tag to the ear or antler as required by state regulation. Next, I'll take a few minutes to admire my hard-won trophy, pausing just a moment to appreciate the beautiful animal that has been the object of off-season dreaming and many hours of travel, preparation, anxiety and effort. Any deer is a hard-earned trophy and worthy of a moment of introspective reflection. For most hunters, success in the deer woods is a long time coming. Savor the moment every chance you get!

NOW, LET'S GET TO WORK!

Gutting Your Deer

Tasty, palatable venison depends on what you do once your deer is down, and there is no time to waste. Your bullet did some internal damage to the animal, and death begins a process of deterioration that must be managed.

The first thing to do is gut the animal. Gutting a deer is not as complicated or "gross" as most people tend to think. The goal is simply to remove all the internal organs from end to end. This removes most of the blood from the animal, shot-damaged tissue and debris that may have leaked into the body cavity from damaged organs, the stomach or intestines.

The process can be confusing to a first-timer who may not even know where to begin, but, on a bet some years ago, I completely gutted a large Maine buck in 56 seconds — it's not a particularly difficult procedure if you know what you are doing.

The gutting process is as varied as the number of hunters who perform the task, and I have seen it done many ways. It's not important how you do it. It's simply important to empty the animal of its viscera in order to halt the bacterial process and help cool the remaining meat.

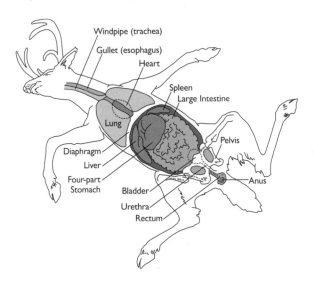

Here's one way to do it:
1. **With the deer laying on its side, lift the tail and "core" the anus just as you would an apple.** Pull the anus upward and insert your knife blade to the hilt about an inch

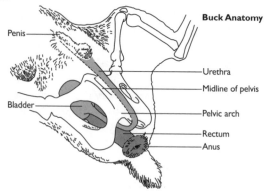

Buck Anatomy

Penis

Urethra

Midline of pelvis

Bladder

Pelvic arch

Rectum

Anus

away from the opening. Now, cut around the anus, gently pulling the anus away from the body as you go. This separates the end of the digestive tract from the body, making it easier to remove the entrails later.

2. **Lay the animal on its back with the shoulders slightly higher than the hind-quarters.** You may need to move the animal to another location to accomplish this. In most areas the ground is uneven so there's rarely a lack of elevated ground that can be used. You may prop the animal on a rock, log or even your backpack, just as long as the shoulders are above the hips. Straddle the carcass facing the animal's head and run your free hand down the breast bone until you can feel the beginning of the soft abdominal wall. This is usually the area

Doe Anatomy

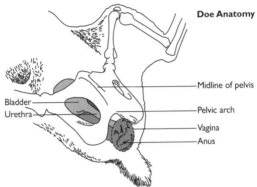

Midline of pelvis

Bladder

Urethra

Pelvic arch

Vagina

Anus

where the black-haired breast and white belly fur join. Press down firmly with one hand and insert the knife blade to the hilt horizontally through the skin and muscle below. Aim the knife point toward the deer's head, not straight down into the body cavity. Doing so will puncture the stomach or intestines, creating interesting sights, smells and sounds most hunters prefer to avoid! Cut forward as far as your knife will go (just an inch or two) creating a hole in the hide through the skin and abdominal muscles. This is the start of your belly cut.

3. **Turn and straddle the carcass with your feet placed on either side of the deer's shoulders, steadying the carcass.** Place two fingers of your free hand into the initial cut. Pull up sharply, and you will create a

small space between the belly muscle and the stomach. Carefully insert the tip of your knife blade into the hole between your fingers, blade up. Moving the knife and your fingers as one unit, slice carefully straight ahead down the center of the belly to a point midway between the rear legs. Your cut should end just beyond the testicles (if it's a buck) or the udder. Work slowly because it's important to keep the abdominal wall away from the stomach and intestines. These organs may protrude slightly as you progress with opening the stomach cavity, but that is normal. Just be sure to keep the knife point and blade away from them!

4. **Straddle the deer again, this time facing the head.** Reach forward inside the carcass along the left and right ribs until you can feel a smooth, red membrane just in front of the stomach. This is the diaphragm, which separates the heart and lungs from the lower digestive system. Move the stomach away from the diaphragm with your free hand and cut along the diaphragm, separating the red membrane from the rib cage. In heart-shot deer, this invariably releases a gush of thick, hot blood, a graphic illustration of why it is not necessary to "bleed" a shot deer by cutting its throat.

5. **Remove your coat or jacket, roll up your sleeves and put on your rubber gloves if you have them.** With your free hand, reach as far up into the chest-neck cavity as you can until you locate the esophagus, a taught, rubbery, hose-like organ. Then, pull your hand out and grip the tip of your knife and work both hands back into the opening. Guide the knife blade to the farthest point of the esophagus you can reach and hold the knife there while your free hand reaches down and grips the esophagus a safe distance away. Maintaining a tight grip, slice through the esophagus and pull the organ back toward yourself. Use the knife to snip away any tendons or muscles that are attached to the ribs or spine. Back away from the deer as you pull making the necessary cuts as you go. In short order the heart, lungs, liver, stomach and intestines will be outside the carcass.

6. **Reach into the rear of the exposed abdominal cavity and pull the pre-cut anal section out of the animal.** You may need to make a few additional cuts here as well. That baseball-sized, creamy white bag you now see is the bladder. Do not puncture the bladder! Find the neck of the bladder with your free hand, pinch it tightly and cut it off above the pinch. Step well away

from the carcass and carefully toss the severed bladder well away from you.

7. **At this point the internal organs have been removed.** You may cut away the reproductive organs if you wish, or wait until the animal is skinned. Reach inside the belly cavity and find the two long, thin, smooth muscles that lay along the spine. These are the tenderloins, the most tender cuts on any animal. Slice either end of each piece and carefully pull the muscle away from the spine. Wash the blood off of the tenderloins and refrigerate as soon as possible.

8. **Move the deer away from the gut pile** and turn the carcass belly-side down with the legs propped open so any blood or material left inside the animal may drain freely. Take a break and let the carcass drain. Pay attention in gathering your equipment and gear. This is where knives, compasses, ammunition and other items end up being lost or misplaced!

It was once traditional to remove the heart and liver to be eaten as a ceremonial dinner in camp the night of a kill, but most states now caution hunters against eating organ meat due to chemical contamination. Check local regulations for cautionary statements regarding game organ consumption advisories.

TRANSPORTING DEER OUT OF THE WOODS

With your deer down, gutted and draining, the next order of business is getting the carcass out of the woods. The goal is to do so without damaging the hide or meat due to excessive dragging or pounding against rocks, logs and other obstacles. If you are hunting alone far from roads or trails there is not much you can do except start dragging, especially in areas where quartering deer prior to tagging is not legal.

Are You Ready For This?

The first thing you must do is admit to yourself that you may not be strong or healthy enough for the task, which involves dragging 100 to 200 pounds of dead weight over rough ground for long periods of time. Hunters who are too old, in poor condition or unaware of their vascular problems die or suffer major heart attacks while dragging deer out of the woods. Be honest about your own physical condition and do not attempt to drag a deer if you have shortness of breath, dizzy spells or chest pains, even occasionally. There are other ways to deal with transporting dead deer, and killing yourself in the process is the least desirable method!

I once shot a buck on a state-designated "primitive area" where no vehicles were allowed. My trophy was over two miles from the nearest gate with elevations varying from 1,100 to 1,400 feet. I was in what I consider the best shape of my life at the time, participating in 10k races several times each year, often running 40 or more miles per week to keep in shape. Most hunters do not walk or run 40 miles per year, and in fact are probably not in very good shape for any kind of physically challenging venture.

In any case, after state foresters refused to allow me (at age 45) to enter the area by vehicle, and with no one else around to help, I elected to drag the deer out on my own. On the way in I had deposited full water bottles about every 200 yards, figuring I'd stop for a break and a drink as I reached each way point. I simply attached a rope to the buck's antlers, turned around and started dragging. Eight hours later I had my deer at the first exit gate where I could drive up and load the buck into my truck. I was exhausted, cut, scratched and bloody but I was alive and the job was done!

Would I do it again? Probably, if there were no other way. Would I recommend it? Definitely not! Hunters I know who have accompanied me to that spot on subsequent trips have told me they would not even want to walk back in there again, let alone go that far while dragging a deer and carrying a pack and rifle!

Dragging Deer By Hand

There was a time when a hunter and his partners would simply grab a deer by its antlers and, through sheer strength of will, drag the animal to the nearest road. Of course, hunting close to roads was always in the game plan, and many hunters refuse to shoot a deer if it were so far back in they'd have trouble getting it out. Hunters today still remark about how they won't hunt certain areas because of the difficulty of dragging a deer back to camp.

The worst way to drag a deer is by hand, using nothing but the antlers or, in the case of a doe, the legs or ears. The bare-handed method is too much work, too inefficient and too rough on the hide and meat. *Avoid hand-dragging if you can!*

The next best technique is to tie a rope around the deer's neck or antlers (with or without the front feet tied in). A deer will "drag" relatively smoothly this way, even smoother if you cut a 12-inch stick and use it for a drag handle. If other people are available, use a longer stick (stout enough for the job) with one or more draggers on each side. The added manpower will make the job much easier.

Adaptations include using shoulder or body harnesses (a shirt or jacket slung diagonally across the chest with lengths of rope tied to the deer), tying the rope around your waist or looping the rope around your forearm.

All of these methods work well on snow, wet leaves or grass. It's still work and will still take some time and effort, but it is easier than dragging a deer through open woods, swamps, brush or clear-cut areas. If possible, avoid dragging your deer down creek bottoms, wet or dry. The terrain in such places is wet, slippery, rocky and uneven, often with entangling brush and vegetation. It's true that creek bottoms are at the lowest elevation, but the trade-off is that you'll be dragging your trophy through some of the worst terrain you can imagine!

The nostalgic, deer-on-a-pole approach, in which the deer's legs are tied to a single pole with one hunter on either end, should be illegal! I have tried this technique several times and it seems that no matter what you do the deer swings and sways with the rhythm of the carriers, pounding the pole down into your shoulders and nearly dislocating your hips in the process. It's not easy to find carriers of the same height, speed and build, and so the deer rocks and rolls like a pendulum all the way back to camp. The technique looks great in pictures, but the last time I tried it was over 20 years ago and I still get back spasms just thinking about it!

Slides and Wheeled Aids

Much progress has been made on the inventive side of deer transportation. Plastic sleds, sheaths and the like are designed to surround the carcass in slippery nylon, plastic or rubber, thereby reducing the amount of drag encountered in rough woods. These products work to an extent, but I have found that there is a loss of control as well because they are often too slick – the deer shoots ahead like a bullet or wobbles from side to side as it slides too quickly over every obstacle it encounters. Going uphill, they are fine, but downhill drags can be an adventure.

The best non-motorized way to transport deer over dry ground (you can't beat a canoe if there's a stream or lake nearby!) is with a wheeled cart or wagon. One-wheeled carts work well enough when two hunters can work together, but you will run into balance problems if you try to single-wheel a deer out of the woods on your own. There are many two-wheeled carts on the market that are excellent for transporting deer on even terrain, roads or trails. I usually try to drag my deer to the nearest logging road or trail, and then use my two-wheeled cart for the remainder of the trip.

The secret to transporting a deer with wheeled vehicles (including bicycles) is to tie the deer securely to the cart (including head and feet) so that there is no wobbling or shifting during transport. No matter how you bring your deer out, be sure to tie it down securely and travel so that the antlers and legs are tucked out of the way and don't catch on every sapling, branch and vine along the way.

Motorized Vehicles

The easiest way to transport deer is by vehicle. Simply strap the animal to the deck of the vehicle or load it into the back of the truck and head for home. This is definitely the way to go if the area you're hunting is open to motorized vehicles. Many state forests, wildlife management areas and state parks do not allow such vehicles, but in many cases you can drag your deer to the nearest unrestricted road and then transport it by vehicle to camp or your car or truck.

Use Caution With Potential Mounts!

No matter how you decide to transport your deer, use extra caution if you intend to have the animal mounted. Do not tie ropes or cords around the deer's head, neck or shoulder region. Damage done to deer hair cannot be repaired by a taxidermist, and if the damage is severe it may require the use of a substitute cape, adding to the cost of the mount.

Also, do not drag the deer. Most taxidermists recommend that you carry it out of the woods to avoid damaging the hide or hair, which of course means a more complicated, time-consuming job. I have participated in a few "deer carries," and it is not easy. The finished product is certainly worth the effort, but plan on having at least four helpers and double the amount of time it would normally take to drag a deer to a road or trail.

To transport a deer meant for mounting, bring a 10x12 tarp and two 12-foot poles. Wrap the poles into the 12-foot length of the tarp to create a stretcher. Tie the wrapped sides tight so they don't unravel enroute. Place the deer on the tarp and, with two carriers per side, head for the road! It would help to have a fifth person walking ahead with an axe or brush cutter to trim away saplings and branches, creating a trail that can accommodate four carriers, a deer and a stretcher. It sounds like a tough job, and it is, but it's worth the effort if you want an exceptional mounting job.

Retrace Your Steps

Most hunters I've known who shot a deer and dragged it out, alone or with friends, end up leaving something of his personal gear behind at the gutting site. I've gone back for other hunters and have recovered hats, gloves, knives and packs. It's always worth returning to the scene, without a gun and with no other agenda but to recover lost equipment. One year I left a stainless steel pocket saw in the woods. I remembered it halfway home and had to wait a full year before I could go back to find it. I knew exactly where it was and found it there the following November, dusty and dirty but none the worse for wear.

Go back and look again — good advice for you and for me!

13. BUTCHERING YOUR OWN DEER

It's a safe bet that most deer hunters enjoy the sport for a number of reasons, not the least of which is the supply of lean, tender venison that ends up in the freezer after a successful trip. Too often, however, the meat stays in the freezer all year and, sometime before the next season; it is given away, fed to the dogs or, worse, thrown into the trash because no one in the family likes the "gamey" taste of venison.

I have been eating venison almost exclusively in home-cooked meals for over 40 years. For 12 years beginning in 1975 I lived in Maine without running water or electricity and if I didn't eat deer and other wild game I didn't eat! I'd shoot a buck or doe sometime in late November, hang the carcass high in a tree outside my cabin door. If it was an exceptionally big deer, come March I'd have to start eating a lot faster because the meat that was left would begin to thaw!

The first year of my self-imposed homesteading exile I ran into the "gamey" problem, which was solved for me by a local woodsman. Carleton Reynolds was not a butcher, but he knew the reason for the strong flavor and waxy after-taste of wild venison, which he mentioned to me the first time I had him over for venison steaks.

"You musta forgot to cut the fat off it," was all he said, but the look on his face spoke volumes. He later explained that the reason folks hated the taste of venison was because they (like me) had butchered the deer as if it were farm-grown beef, cutting it up fat and all, even using the strong-tasting tallow when grinding the odd cuts and scraps for burger.

For better-tasting venison, keep these basic rules in mind:

- Remove all fat from venison!
- Do not use venison fat for ground meat!
- Mix beef or pork fat with your lean, fat-trimmed venison.

MAKING MEAT

To be honest, the easiest way to process a deer for the table is to hire the services of an experienced butcher. Many independent commercial processors will do the job, and sometimes a butcher working for the local grocery store will take care of the job. Expect to spend anywhere from $50 to $100 for meat processing, which should include skinning, packaging and labeling. It's the way to go if you do not have the time, tools or facilities for the job. Just be sure the butcher removes all the fat from the meat and adds beef or pork fat to burger and sausage.

If you plan to skin, butcher and package your own deer, plan to spend three or four hours in the process, more if you have never done the job before. Nothing about meat processing is mysterious or difficult, but it is time-consuming and like painting the living room, it can create more of a mess than you expected!

There are several ways to skin a deer, but all

have one thing in common – the hide must come off! Some hunters hang the deer head up; some hang the animal by its hocks (head down). Many Western hunters skin their deer on the ground in the field, quartering the animal for transport home. Choose your method and proceed. If you are going to have your deer's head mounted, contact a taxidermist to see how he wants you to skin the animal and proceed as directed. That process is different from skinning the animal for meat processing!

To make the job easier, hang the deer in a cool place out of the wind and weather. A garage or shed is perfect – there will be hair flying, bits of meat and fat to discard, etc., so keep a plastic bucket or trash barrel handy. Also, keep several sharp knives nearby, and a hone or sharpener. Nothing dulls a knife quicker than skinning a deer!

With the animal elevated, we're ready to begin. Let's assume the animal is hanging head up, with the throat about as high as you can reach.

1. **Begin by extending the belly cut straight up over the brisket and chest to the point where the neck meets the head.** Cut slowly in an upward motion – do not cut from the hair side in or hack at the hide because this dislodges hair that will stick to the exposed meat like glue. Take your time!

2. **When you reach the head-neck juncture, stop.** Now, pull the hide on one side of the chest toward you and make another

cut from the brisket along the inside of one leg all the way to the first joint. Do this for all four legs.

3. **Next, cut the hide around each leg joint and around the head at the throat.** Go slowly, work from the meat side with the knife blade up, and try to avoid getting hair stuck to the exposed meat. Use care now or plan to spend long periods of time picking the hair off the meat later! (The hair must come off or it will taint the flavor of the meat!)

4. **At this point you have cut around the head, out to and around all four legs.** Now you can begin to remove the hide. Reach up to the highest point where the hide has been cut (the throat), grab a corner of the skin and begin pulling downward. On warm deer the hide will come away easily. If your deer has been dead for several days, it may require some effort. If the deer is partially frozen, the hide will fight you every inch of the way.

5. **This is the place for a dull knife with a broad, stout blade.** You should never have to cut and hack to get a deer's hide off the carcass. Simply pull down on the hide and use the dull blade to pry the hide away from difficult areas as you encounter them. If you see bits of red meat adhering to the hide, pry the hide

away to avoid stripping a layer of good meat away from the carcass.

6. **In general, the hide will pull away slowly but steadily.** You may encounter trouble spots in the brisket area and near the rump, but in most areas the hide will come off easily. Work slowly, avoid getting hair on the exposed meat and do not make any cuts in the skin – the entire hide should come off the deer in one piece.

7. **Problems may arise when you reach the lower end of the deer, especially if the deer's back feet are touching the floor.** If possible, raise the animal higher so you don't end up with a "puddle" of hide wrapped around the back legs. It is much easier to pull downward on the hide than to be bent over and trying to push it off the last few inches of the carcass.

8. **Cut off the tail when you reach it, using a sharp knife or meat saw to sever the tailbone close to the rump.** When finished, you should have a skinned carcass before you, head and lower legs still encased in fur, and a complete hide, tail attached, on the floor.

You can have the hide tanned, made into leather or you can simply discard it. If you know of someone who ties fishing flies, offer them the tail and white belly fur in exchange for some flies or streamers!

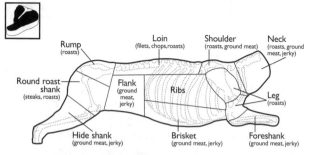

BASIC CUTS

With the hide off the deer, spend some time cutting away all bloodshot areas, blackened meat, bone chips, fatty tissue or anything else that is not clean, lean red meat. These are the things that taint the flavor of venison.

Next, it's time to cut the carcass into manageable pieces. What you do here depends on your personal meal preferences. You can butcher the animal as if it were a beef cow, processing it into steaks, chops roasts and burger, but at this point you've probably noticed . . . there's not as much meat on a skinned deer as you thought! In many areas of the South, for example, the average adult deer weights 60 pounds with the head, hide and legs removed!

If possible, chill or partially freeze deer meat before cutting. This makes the cutting process much easier. In the North, it's normal to hang a deer for a week or more before processing. In warmer climes, hanging the deer (or skinned meat) in a cooler at about 40 degrees will improve its flavor, palatability and workability. Warm, fresh venison is soft, mushy and very difficult to handle.

Decide how you want to process the animal. *Consider your options and make your decision before you start cutting and packaging.*

If possible, work on a solid tabletop with hot water and a sink nearby. To begin, set out several trays or pans nearby, as many sharp knives as you own, freezer paper, air-tight plastic bags or a vacuum sealer, and labeling tools (tape, indelible markers, etc.). *Do not package deer meat without labeling it!* This is the law in some states but it's also the sensible thing to do.

With your work space ready to go, it's time to start butchering!

1. **To begin, cut the unskinned portion of the legs off the deer.** Cut into the meat around the legs with a knife and then cut the bones using a meat saw. Save the legs for interesting mounts – gun racks, lamps and the like. Simply toss the legs into a freezer and deal with them later. They'll keep just fine frozen.

2. **Now you have a skinned, legless carcass hanging in front of you.** To make the butchering job easier, I cut off smaller pieces of the deer as it hangs and work from them. The normal process is to cut the head and neck off, and then split the carcass down the spine to create two halves of the animal. However, I have found this to be too much meat for one man to handle, very difficult to make the necessary cuts.

3. **I start by cutting off the hind quarters.**
Make a knife cut entirely around the spine
just above the rump. Using the meat saw,
cut the quarters off by sawing through the
spine. This leaves you with both hindquarters in hand and the carcass still hanging.

4. **Place the hindquarters on a solid surface,
rump side up.** Using a knife, cut through
the center of the quarters top to bottom
and around to the other side, severing the
pelvis. With the quarters rump side up
again, use the meat saw to cut down the
spine, separating the two quarters.

5. **Trim away all fat, tendons and other
loose ends and discard.** Never add "white"
venison scraps, bones or marrow to meat
you intend to eat! This is where that dread-
ed gamey flavor is derived.

6. **With a clean, trimmed quarter in front
of you, begin cutting away your first
steaks using a long, sharp knife.** A beef
butcher would use a meat saw and include
the leg bone but this might spread bone
marrow which imparts a gamey flavor.

7. **You should be able to get 8 or 10 steaks
out of each hind quarter depending
upon the thickness of the cut.** Trim away
the remaining meat for burger or stew
meat, as you prefer.

8. **Package your cuts as you make them.**
It's best to package meat in servings for

two even if you have a large family. Small batches freeze quickly and evenly, while larger packages take longer to freeze.

9. **Next, I fillet the backstraps away from the backbone.** In the meat-processing world, these are the chops and prime rib of the animal, it's excellent meat!

10. **To cut the backstrap away from the spine, insert the tip of a sharp knife along the spine at a point between the shoulders.** You should see a "pattern" where this long, strip of meat begins. Cut along the spine on either side all the way to the point where the hindquarters were severed. Fillet the backstrap from the spine and ribs in one long piece. Do this on both sides. You will end up with two strips of lean, boneless backstrap that can be cut into individual steak medallions, two or three small roasts or left whole.

11. **Simply raise the shoulder by the "arm" and cut close to the ribs all around the shoulder.** Shoulder meat may be cut into steaks or stew meat. Cut and trim as you desire, but be sure to discard all fat and tendons.

12. **At this point you're left with a neck with carcass attached.** I normally cut away the remaining scraps of lean, red meat from the neck and carcass and have it mixed with beef or pork made into burger or sausage.

14. YOUR TROPHY BUCK

Hopefully, every deer you shoot will be a trophy worthy of mounting. Taxidermists around the world stress the need for immediate field care of game destined for mounting, and too often a poor mounting job is the result of the hunter's ignorance, laziness or lack of preparation.

Ideally, your trophy should travel from the woods to the tagging station to the taxidermist. If you can get the animal to the shop the same day it was killed you'll have a mount that is as close to perfect as you can get it. The taxidermist will skin the animal himself so that he has plenty of skin to work with and a minimum of patching and sewing to do during the mounting process.

There are things you can do to improve the quality of a mount.

Follow these simple rules of trophy care!

1. Call your taxidermist before the hunt and ask him how he would like the head and cape handled.
2. Never cut an animal's throat! As you will have seen from the gutting process, there is no need to "bleed" a gunshot deer!
3. Do not drag a potential mount out of the woods. This can damage or remove hair from the cape.
4. Do not hang your trophy buck by the neck using ropes, chains, straps or anything else that may damage the hide.
5. Bring the animal to the taxidermist as soon as possible after it is killed. If the trophy

can't be brought to the taxidermist within 24 hours, the cape and antlers should be salted (using ordinary table salt – figure on five pounds of salt per hide), placed inside two heavy plastic bags and then frozen for transport to the shop.

If you want to do your own caping and skinning, contact the taxidermist first and learn how he wants the job done. Some taxidermists are satisfied with the standard behind-the-shoulders skinning, but others have innovative ways to remove the hide. Follow the taxidermist's instructions and deliver your trophy as soon as possible.

Expect the average deer mount to take six months to a year to complete. Some mounts can be turned around in a few weeks, but for production-line work, expect your head to return sometime around the beginning of next deer season.

When considering a taxidermist, keep in mind that it may be better to hire a shop near where you killed the deer rather than your hometown taxidermist. Some shops specialize in fish, birds or small game rather than deer, or they may do relatively few deer. Talk to the taxidermist, examine his work and make your decision based on what you see.

When you find a taxidermist whose work you admire, get his contact information and details on how he'd like to see deer heads handled and delivered. The more you can do to help your taxidermist the better the final mount will be.

HOW DOES YOUR BUCK MEASURE UP?

In many areas of the country, primarily the Northeast, "trophy" bucks are still classed by weight rather than antler score, although that long-held tradition is slowly losing ground. The trend now is to measure and compare antler scores, either as "typical" growth (even points on both sides with a normal, symmetrical configuration), or "non-typical," with many odd points, drop tines and bizarre formations that can be difficult to measure and impossible to describe.

In many states, the trend in certain areas and

counties is toward "quality deer management" (QDM), which in most cases means bucks with antlers of four or more points on at least one side or with antler spreads at least wider than the deer's ears (or about 16 inches).

The majority of deer taken by hunters are does, young bucks or average 8-pointers. Very few of

the deer taken each year are considered "trophy" bucks by Boone & Crockett standards (minimum score of 160 typical or 180 non-typical). Most hunters utilizing public lands may never see a single "qualifier" in their lifetimes. Most trophy-class whitetails are found in areas where hunting pressure is low, habitat is exceptional (a good mix of farmlands and woodlots) and abbreviated muzzleloader or shotgun seasons only.

In a nutshell, it takes prime habitat, a mild climate, genetics (a propensity for bucks to grow trophy antlers) and time — bucks of trophy size are generally 4½ to 7½ years old. When most of the deer harvest consists of immature bucks, it follows that few are likely to live long enough to develop trophy-sized antlers. If the habitat is marginal, important nutritional factors are missing. Include harsh winters, poor genetics and long rifle seasons and it's easy to understand why some areas will never produce trophy deer.

Bucks living in highly-restricted areas of the East and South do have time to grow large antlers, but most of these exceptional deer are rarely taken by hunters because of local laws banning hunting; or because private landowners will not allow access. To find out more about the Boone & Crockett Club or how to measure deer antlers for official score see the charts in the Appendix or, log onto www.booneandcrockett.com.

LAST FLAG

It is hoped that this little book has been helpful in your quest for venison this year. Do what needs to be done to place yourself in the "right place at the right time" and be ready when your opportunity arises. What happens now is up to you. Give what you've learned a chance to work. Tough it out when the woods seem empty and all the shooting seems to be taking place on the other side of the hill. Maintain a positive attitude and enter the woods each day with enthusiasm and vigor. Get up in the morning knowing the deer are out there. All you have to do is find them!

Be ready and be vigilant. Clear your mind of everything but the crunch of dry leaves and the snap and crackle of brittle twigs. Wait for that clean, broadside shot behind the shoulder, squeeze the trigger and ... he's yours! Welcome to the club!

WHITETAIL DEER AT A GLANCE

Species: *Odocoileus virginianus*

Geographic Range: Southern Canada and most of the continental United States, except New Mexico, Arizona and southern California. Their range extends throughout Central America to Bolivia.

Habitat: Whitetail deer thrive in a variety of habitats ranging from the northern boreal forests to southern saw grass and hammock swamps. Habitats include a wide range including developed suburbs, farmlands, dense forest, scrub forest, swamplands, brush regions, chaparral and cactus and thorn-brush deserts. Ideal habitat contains good cover and nutrient-rich food sources.

Weight (Adult): 125 - 300 lbs.   **Length (Adult):** 62 - 86 inches

Coloration: Generally a gray shade in winter and redder in summer. White fur found in a band behind the nose, around the eyes, over the chin and throat, on the inner upper legs and belly.

Reproduction: Season—October to December, fawns are born in the spring. Interval—once yearly.

Expected Lifespan: 10 years in the wild—average 2 years.

Behavior: Whitetail deer are nervous, shy, and extremely agile, able to bound at speeds of up to 30 miles per hour over tangled ground. Whitetail home ranges are generally small, often a half-mile square or less. Whitetails are generally solitary, especially in summer. The basic social unit is a female and her fawns, although does will graze together and bucks occasionally form transient groups which disband before the rut. Whitetail deer are not especially vocal, although disturbed adults make a variety of whistles or snorts. White-tailed deer have scent glands their feet and on the outer and inner hind legs which are used for communcation.

Food Habits: Whitetail deer feed mainly from before dawn to several hours after and from late afternoon until dusk. They browse on the twigs, leaves, shrubs, acorns, fungi, grasses and herbs that are available in their habitat. These include buds and twigs of maple, sassafras, dogwood, poplar, aspen and birch as well as undergrowth such as honeysuckle, sumac, wintergreen, greenbriar, bearberry, witch-hazel, hawthorn, wood sorrel and even poison ivy. In the fall, depending on region, they feed on mast—fallen acorns and beech nuts (white oak acorns are a favorite) and fruit (persimmons). Conifers are eaten in winter when other foods are scarce. Of cultivated crops, corn, alfalfa, clovers, cabbage, soybeans, and rye are all consumed. In desert areas, plants such as huajillo brush, yucca, prickly pear cactus and various shrubs may be the main elements of whitetail diet. Evidence has recorded the consumption of well over 700 species of plants in North America by white-tailed deer.

POPULAR DEER CARTIDGES

Range at which cartridges retain 1200 ft-lbs of energy

Cartrigdge	Bullet Weight (grams)	Muzzle Velocity	1200 Ft/lbs. (yards)
.243 Winchester	100	2960	250
.243 WSM	100	3110	300
.25-06 Remington	120	2990	360
.270 Winchester	130	3060	390
.270 Winchester	150	2850	295
.270 WSM	150	3150	450
.280 Remington	150	2970	435
.280 Remington	160	2840	500
7mm-08 Remington	140	2860	400
7mm WSM	150	3200	500
7mm Remington Mag.	150	3110	485
7mm Remington Mag.	175	2860	575
7mm Remington UM	140	3424	500
.30-30 Winchester	170	2200	140
.308 Winchester	150	2910	435
.308 Winchester	180	2620	425
.30-06 Springfield	150	2910	435
.30-06 Springfield	180	2700	460
.300 WSM	150	3300	500
.300 Remington SA	150	3450	500
.300 Winchester Mag.	180	2960	645
.375 Winchester	200	2200	175
.45-70 Government	300	1880	225

BOONE AND CROCKETT CLUB: TYPICAL WHITETAIL TROPHY SCORES

TYPICAL WHITETAIL AND COUES' DEER

MINIMUM SCORES

	AWARDS	ALL-TIME
whitetail	160	170
Coues'	100	110

KIND OF DEER
☐ whitetail
☐ Coues'

Detail of a point measurement

A. Right_____ **A.** Left _____ No. of points

B. _____ Tip to Tip Spread

C. _____ Greatest Spread

D. _____ Inside Spread

SPREAD CREDIT _____
Spread Credit May Equal But Not Exceed Longer Main Beam

SUBTOTALS
TOTAL TO E

Add the Spread Credit to the totals for the right and left antlers. Subtract the difference total for the Final Score

TOTALS
Spread Credit _____
R-Antler _____
L-Antler _____
Subtotal _____
– Difference _____
Final Score _____

Right ABNORMAL POINTS Left

	R-Antler	L-Antler	Difference
E			
F			
G-1			
G-2			
G-3			
G-4			
G-5			
G-6			
G-7			
H-1			
H-2			
H-3			
H-4			
TOTALS			

INSTRUCTIONS FOR MEASURING TYPICAL WHITETAIL AND COUES'

A. Number of Points on Each Antler: To be counted a point, the projection must be at least one inch long, with length exceeding width at one inch or more of length. All points are measured from the nearest edge of beam, over the outer curve, to the tip as illustrated. Beam tip is counted as a point but not measured as a point.

B. Tip to Tip Spread is measured between tips of main beams.

C. Greatest Spread is measured between perpendiculars at a right angle to the center line of the skull at widest part, whether across main beams or points.

D. Inside Spread of Main Beams is measured at a right angle to the center line of the skull at widest point between main beams. Enter this measurement again as the Spread Credit if it is less than or equal to the length of the longer main beam; if greater, enter longer main beam length for Spread Credit.

E. Total of Lengths of all Abnormal Points: Abnormal Points are those nontypical in location (such as points originating from a point or from bottom or sides of main beam) or extra points beyond normal pattern of points. Measure in usual manner and record in appropriate blanks.

F. Length of Main Beam is measured from the center of the lowest outside edge of burr over the outer side to the most distant point of the main beam. The point of beginning is that point on the burr where the center line along the outer side of the beam intersects the burr, then following generally the line of the illustration.

G-1-2-3-4-5-6-7. Length of Normal Points: Normal points project from the top or front of the main beam in the general pattern illustrated. They are measured from nearest edge of main beam over outer curve to tip. Lay the cable/tape along the outer curve of the beam so that the bottom edge of the cable/tape coincides with the top edge of the beam on both sides of point to determine the baseline for point measurement. Record point lengths in appropriate blanks.

H-1-2-3-4. Circumferences are taken as detailed in illustration for each measurement.

To have your trophy officially scored you can locate a B&C Official Measurer in your area by contacting the Club through our website www.booneandcrockettclub.com or call (406)542-1888

BOONE AND CROCKETT CLUB: NON-TYPICAL WHITETAIL TROPHY SCORES

NON-TYPICAL WHITETAIL AND COUES' DEER

MINIMUM SCORES

	AWARDS	ALL-TIME
whitetail	185	195
Coues'	105	120

KIND OF DEER
- ❏ whitetail
- ❏ Coues'

Detail of a point measurement

Right **ABNORMAL POINTS** Left

A. Right _____ **A.** Left _____ No. of points

B. _____ Tip to Tip Spread

C. _____ Greatest Spread

D. _____ Inside Spread

SPREAD CREDIT _____
Spread Credit May Equal But Not
Exceed Longer Main Beam

SUBTOTALS
TOTAL TO E

Add the Spread Credit to the
totals for the right and left
antlers. Subtract the difference then add E (abnormal
points) for the Final Score

TOTALS

Spread Credit _____
R-Antler _____
L-Antler _____
Subtotal _____
− Difference _____
Subtotal _____
+ E _____
Final Score _____

	R-Antler	L-Antler	Difference
F			
G-1			
G-2			
G-3			
G-4			
G-5			
G-6			
G-7			
H-1			
H-2			
H-3			
H-4			
TOTALS			

INSTRUCTIONS FOR MEASURING NON-TYPICAL WHITETAIL AND COUES'

A. Number of Points on Each Antler: To be counted a point, the projection must be at least one inch long, with length exceeding width at one inch or more of length. All points are measured from the nearest edge of beam, over the outer curve, to the tip as illustrated. Beam tip is counted as a point but not measured as a point.

B. Tip to Tip Spread is measured between tips of main beams.

C. Greatest Spread is measured between perpendiculars at a right angle to the center line of the skull at widest part, whether across main beams or points.

D. Inside Spread of Main Beams is measured at a right angle to the center line of the skull at widest point between main beams. Enter this measurement again as the Spread Credit if it is less than or equal to the length of the longer main beam; if greater, enter longer main beam length for Spread Credit.

E. Total of Lengths of all Abnormal Points: Abnormal Points are those non-typical in location (such as points originating from a point or from bottom or sides of main beam) or extra points beyond normal pattern of points. Measure in usual manner and record in appropriate blanks.

F. Length of Main Beam is measured from the center of the lowest outside edge of burr over the outer side to the most distant point of the main beam. The point of beginning is that point on the burr where the center line along the outer side of the beam intersects the burr, then following generally the line of the illustration.

G-1-2-3-4-5-6-7. Length of Normal Points: Normal points project from the top or front of the main beam in the general pattern illustrated. They are measured from nearest edge of main beam over outer curve to tip. Lay the cable/tape along the outer curve of the beam so that the bottom edge of the cable/tape coincides with the top edge of the beam on both sides of point to determine the baseline for point measurement. Record point lengths in appropriate blanks.

H-1-2-3-4. Circumferences are taken as detailed in illustration for each measurement.

To have your trophy officially scored you can locate a B&C Official Measurer in your area by contacting the Club through our website www.booneandcrockettclub.com or call (406) 542-1888

IRON SIGHTS

Changing The Point Of Impact

1. Shot is low and left.

2. Move front sight down and left or move rear sight up and right.

3. Sights will now be centered on point of impact.

4. Subsequent shots should be or target.

Adjusting Open Sights

- To move the line of sight DOWN (shot strikes BELOW the point of aim) the REAR sight is RAISED.
- To move the line of sight UP (shot strikes ABOVE the point of aim) the REAR sight is LOWERED.
- To move the line of sight LEFT (shot strikes LEFT of the point of aim) the REAR sight is moved RIGHT.
- To move the line of sight RIGHT (shot strikes RIGHT of the point of aim) the REAR sight is moved LEFT.